AERON BERGMAN
ALEJANDRA SALINAS

TELEPATHY
传心术

W9-CYB-185

D

INCA Press

For Agnes Bergman-Salinas

TABLE OF CONTENTS

TELEPATHY
传心术

The power of definition is critical ground — a location to take a stand. Every epoch, school of thought, university art program, art scene, and journalistic cohort generates a cluster of assumptions about what art is meant to be and how it will fit into an existing ecosystem. The concept of art depends on the social matrix. During the turmoil of the twentieth century Adorno attempted to negotiate art, society, ethics, and aesthetics when he wrote: "The concept of art is located in a historically changing constellation of elements; it refuses definition."[1] Art refuses definition and as soon as it is defined, it cements an historical moment that immediately ends. It is open not only to the wide and stunning range of human imagination and historical tides: its indeterminacy also leaves it wide open for hijacking.

ART IN THE ENTROPIC FIELD

The consequence of the victory of Duchamp, Cage, (et. al) and their gestures of transubstantiation, is that contemporary art has expanded to include anything and everything, and has stretched itself so thin that it is now almost nothing but the procedures of management. This tradition is harmonious with the legalist doctrines implementing the social Darwinism of neoliberalism. In order to differentiate, promote, and determine the difference between contemporary art and say social work, cooking, dancing, education, landscape architecture, clothing design, industrial design, music videos, fashion magazines, colonialism, astrophysics, and so on, then legalist, institutional authorization clears up any categorical ambiguity declared symbolically. Art institutions determine what is art, and who represents and thus is the beneficiary of each klepto-maneuver and stylistic turn of the private appropriation — theft — of public wealth, knowledge, and every atom in the universe.

Art is determined by power, which is determined by brute force in the form of a violent social class backed by courts, rabid police forces and militarized control of resources. Art plays the symbolic role of colonizing absolutely every object and human activity, demonstrating and normalizing that the universe is administered by the upper-middle class, and owned by the ruling class. Contemporary art is not in opposition to this fact, it is formed by this fact.

NEW VOCABULARY

Those without legal rights to speak, move, or appropriate, must invent new vocabulary on these margins. A wide majority senses exclusionary pay-to-play enforced by jargon – and armed guards – and declare art hopelessly elitist. But even if it is tempting to give up art as a plaything for the rich, and focus instead purely on activism, this is a terrible development: everyone owns equal stakes in art, in knowledge, the resources of earth, and in the future. Value must be corrected to deflate the massive overvaluation of the ruling class. We need a new vocabulary that is inclusive, instead of simplistic, sloganeering, careerist condescension! Our present is flooded with the ideology that has melted hope and permafrost. The future will be better only if we index doubt and dispel delusion, leaving behind traces of this struggle. New vocabulary could adopt excluded and ignored histories, if improvised, agency-generated conditions embrace changing constellations of elements based on facts on the ground instead of ideologies in the air. Any new concepts for art should absolutely not contain any variation of the word "modern" in it, and anything "post" arrives dead. New art words will not be reduced to "isms" because that is a seasonal variation of the same necro-monument. New concepts will reset value, dispelling the extreme violence of control, the worship of the attention economy, gamed exchange, fathomless greed, indifference to life, and speculation funnelled through the mythical merit system. New vocabulary will emphasize and celebrate life. New words will recognize the heart, now, in a present that connects past with future. Otherness and the unspeakable melancholy of consciousness will be stirred by working with life, speculating on a long future on earth for our children and children's children. Such words will assist in the overthrow of the blasé market that destroys love, solidarity, potential, thought, and life.

Unsettled refugees and conscious malcontents of neoliberal, vile-maxim capitalism fight for scraps of potential against constructions disguised as natural sciences. We need refreshed insights from MLK armed with the collective intellect, and a will to collaborate. We need vocabulary that emanates and radiates, instead of soaking us up like the reeking, mouldy sponge of colonialism. We need words that model the material present with the same facility as modelling a future. We need words that define the essential human action of existing in, facing, and coping with every new moment.

传心术, TELEPATHY.

The word telepathy has a Greek origin that we prefer to de-emphasize (because that would demonstrate typical scholarly laziness and western hegemony). Rather, we draw from its Chinese translation. It is pronounced: chuán xīn shù, and it means more-or-less telepathy. However, it becomes more interesting when we break down the three characters:

传 summon; propagate, transmit

心 heart; mind, intelligence; soul

术 art, skill, special feat; method, technique

The plasticity of chuán xīn shù is apparent. The three characters individually generate a complex and provocative scenario that actively marginalizes institution — the action it describes does not depend on a structure of dubious legitimation. The action only needs two souls and an expanse for it to be complete. This new use of the word telepathy is a nod to science fiction, however it does not stumble into faith-based fantasy or magic. Telepathy 传心术 emphasizes the transmission of heart and mind through special feats and methods. Telepathy 传心术 takes into account that the natural world is processed via our sensory organs, speculation grounded by our limitations, and the material. Telepathy, 传心术 is agency, lived experience and hopeful dreaming processed by a soul, transmitted by action or object to or from the present flash.

LIVING MODELS

Bai Juyi 白居易 wrote the poem "Feelings on Watching the Moon" in the 6th century AD. The poem springs from a specific, local situation — a politically minded poem with local and personally sentimental concerns. It also carries root meaning and speaks, clearly, 1,170 or so years later. The poem describes how local, power-grabbing social conflict leads to broken lives, broken family binds, and constrained movement when one finds oneself stuck in a violent, hostile, sick society. A broken family is united only when gazing at the moon together, ten thousand li apart, connected by a scientific reference point. Site specificity and soul compress into one efficient time-capsule form, linking an individual and their environment with a continuous present, using a familiar rock in heavy orbit. Both in form and content, especially when we consider its calligraphic delivery, the work transmits heart and mind through a special method, far outside frames of power that cannot influence how this moment projects into the future.

Consider another historical moment, in the Soviet dream zone between imagination and concrete form — the transition between suprematism and constructivism. When El Lissitzky, Rodchenko and Liubov Popova, etc., crossed from the spiritual, absolute non-objectivity of suprematism over to materialist, utilitarian constructivism: choices were made. However, in a fertile instant of insecurity, unseen and hazy unknown, we recognize the human longing to speculate on consciousness and ethics. Let's focus on one moment: Popova's indecision in 1921 whether to embrace the constructivist's role of state organization of the elements, or to remain in absolute abstraction: freedom or solidarity. Both! If we look closely at her work Study for Space-Force Construction, from 1921, we see a work that refuses to take a predetermined form, and refuses to be framed, a radical openness that communicates possibility and hope deep into the future. The work is an exploration that could, and did, become a painting, a drawing, textile design, graphic design, architecture and a model for life improved. It helps to visualize this work because of its fragile position, because of the way it hesitates. This work is internally unsure of what it is, and hadn't yet been hijacked by the politburo. It displays existential doubt, a moment when a proposed system asserted itself over historical precedent based on the speculation that there could be a better way to live. Popova searched feverishly in the rainbow between pure reason and material reality. This work vibrates beyond formal novelty or historical footnote on the spectrum of electromagnetic radiation.

Telepathy, 传心术 resets value, again and again, like ohm brings the mind back to nothingness, and shift-alt-delete reboots a crashed algorithm. Market value is inflicted upon absolutely every human activity from pre-birth to post-death — from a lone moment of reflective silence to a howl in the crowd. Telepathy, 传心术 resists or at least ignores meaningless value assertions for a few crucial seconds, with a repetitive frequency that may form habit. The ability to dismiss arbitrary and cruel value systems may even become normalized. The forms this may take are unknown and unpredictable. Essential contributions appear, like magic, improbable and wonderful, miracles of consciousness and freedom of movement. We need to recognize and celebrate these moments.

符离及下邽弟妹

时难年饥世业空
弟兄羁旅各西东
田园寥落干戈后
骨肉流离道路中
吊影分为千里雁
辞根散作九秋蓬
共看明月应垂泪
一夜乡心五处同

Feelings on Watching the Moon

The times are hard a year of famine has emptied the fields My brothers live abroad scattered west and east Now fields and gardens are scarcely seen after the fighting Family members wander scattered on the road Attached to shadows like geese ten thousand li apart Or roots uplifted into September's autumn air We look together at the bright moon and then the tears should fall This night our wish for home can make five places one
—Bai Juyi

1. Theodor Adorno, *Aesthetic Theory*
(London: Bloomsbury, 1997), 2.

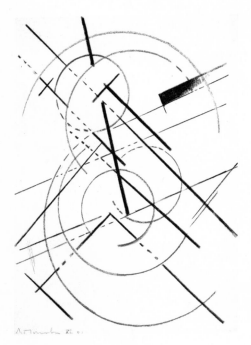

Liubov Popova
Study for Space-Force Construction
1921

ART IN THE AGE OF KLEPTOMANIA

Art is utilized at any point along ideological spectra. It is naïve at best, and more often slight-of-hand, to assume or claim that art weighs heavier on the left, sides with the oppressed, or is socially, intellectually, or critically progressive at its core. Salespeople cynically sell the idea of art's teleology, while gaming its potential as a weapon. Art for art's sake, and other claims of the autonomy of art obfuscate the self-interests of class and power. Looking at the capitals of contemporary art, we see that they are exactly the same capitols of capital, power and insider trading. Over the centuries, art drifted from the service of a church to the service of capital, and it is now fully servile to neoliberal capitalism. It is not coincidence that the rise of the contemporary art brand corresponded exactly with the rise of neoliberalism, both reaching maturity in the 1980's. The most powerful and "important" art follows and reflects power in a precision dance. Mostly everyone in the art ecosystem is keeping busy.

The busy-ness of art is determined by the dominant worldview — predatory neoliberal capitalism — in the same way in which art used to be determined by the cosmology of all-powerful religious bureaucracies. Both are belief systems functioning primarily as hierarchical control protocol. Art in the church, like art in neoliberal capitalism, is utilized to standardize and naturalize strategic images in the collective imagination and thus determine official conduct. Art in the church is sold as visible evidence of scripture. Art in neoliberal capitalism is sold on pragmatic terms, in the infallible market, as evidence of the justness of its competitions.

The busy-ness of art mimes gestures of independence from the dominant ecosystems in the guise of liberal ideals of freedom of speech and freedom of expression. The artist, like the entrepreneur, appears to be free, and is held up as an example of how free (liberal) the society is, thus positioning failure and despair as the fault of the individual. The rhetoric of artistic freedom is in perfect harmony with the rhetoric of the heroic individual thriving in the free market of capitalism. Both artist and entrepreneur thrive on appropriation.

It is not enough to state that art serves capital and move on to frothy, feel-good, redemptive narratives. It is important to understand exactly how and where control occurs in the ecosystem. Colonial forces despoil art. This has always been the case, reflecting the flux of human power. In history, art played normative roles in the service of various liturgical hierarchies, replaced in an endless succession. Presently, the role of art is at the service of normalizing yet another magical belief system. Many words associated with or developed by art and artists have been completely colonized, despoiled by neoliberal business models. Words such as creativity, innovation, and disruption circled (perhaps naively) in art's orbit, (disruption is a classic avant-garde strategy) — but these words have been snatched and employed at the service of private entrepreneurial enterprise such as tech, finance, the military industrial complex, and for-profit health care, education, etc. The image of the lone, fearless artist, blazing ahead of social norms, the ideal individualist, has become the mythical figure of today's alpha "creative" the ruthless entrepreneur. Ayn Rand used and expanded this myth in her book The Fountainhead. Notably, her hero Howard Roark, a "creative," was partially modeled after a serial killer who kidnapped, raped, dismembered and murdered a little girl, about whom she wrote in awe: "A man who really stands alone, in action and in soul."[1] The psychopathy observed in the serial killer, and at least simulated by Rand herself, has been normalized society-wide as the ideal way of living and acting in social relations. Serving as a scriptural normalization of psychopathy and extreme selfishness, outspoken Rand adepts are currently well positioned across government, industry, the supreme court, education and of course, the art ecosystem.[2] It is essential to locate where, how, and when this has happened, and what role art has played in its implementation in order to unravel it.

OPPOSITION?

In the 21st century there are very few fields that develop and utilize value systems parallel to the ruling theology of today: neoliberal capitalism. Two prominent fields that are sometimes capable of such opposition are religion (irony of ironies) and science (not the corporate version.)

Examples of religious opposition to neoliberal capitalism include Pope Francis' statement to the Wall Street Journal that "capitalism is terrorism against all humanity."[3] Rabbi Jonathan Sacks also spoke out: "Humanity was not created to serve markets. Markets were created to serve humankind."[4] Another powerful example of religious opposition is the Sharia compliant Islamic finance system practiced by Iran, Malaysia, and the countries of the Gulf Cooperation Council, a growing banking system outlawing rent-seeking via usury, or "riba."[5]

In science, perhaps the strongest opposition to neoliberal capitalism is seen in the scientific consensus on climate change summed up in this statement on the website of NASA: "Observations throughout the world make it clear that climate change is occurring, and rigorous scientific research demonstrates that the greenhouse gases emitted by human activities are the primary driver."[6] These human activities are primarily driven by capitalism, enforced by neoliberal legislation.

Many artists and art professionals assume that art is somehow opposed to neoliberalism by default. This denies the important interdisciplinary work of diffusion, the role of art in image making, and the recuperative reflex of the system. Meaningful and sincere opposition in art is weakened and absorbed in the wake of the art ecosystem's non-stop global party that simply invites its most visible critics to join in the fun. Most of the work and atmosphere in the public displays of contemporary art are celebratory, super-sized, corporate sponsored parodies of opposition via the marriage of art, the experience economy, and entrepreneurialism. Artists are revered more for success in itself, and their subsequent super Rand-size egos, than for any content, critical or conformist, their work may or may not hold. Even art that is openly critical of values such as capitalism, racism, greed, war, poverty, and exploitation is welcomed to the party as long as it takes the form of the ritualistic absolution of the sins of the global ruling class and their obedient managerial class. Art in its contemporary form has little oppositional relevance because of its honoured place at the dinner party.[7] And finally, the extreme inequality of access and resources among artists is an exact reflection of the extreme inequality of opportunity in society, and is held up exactly this way to be a fact of nature, thus normalizing the current construction of society.

INDIVIDUAL ARTISTS ARE NOT THE CAUSE OR SOLUTION

If the responsibility weighs too heavily on the artist to retake art from the horrible norms of neoliberalism, then we must not press them too much. Privatising failure and guilt is another normalizing policy of neoliberalism. It is easy to scapegoat the individual artist and a dreadful, blatantly propagandistic, or impotent work of art, when the problem is the ecosystem. When artists are well adjusted in order to compete for the resources necessary for life, then we should not begrudge people their survival instincts, escape mechanisms, and will-to-dominate. But we must also not venerate market conformists, or hold up realist, centrist, careerists as today's most valuable contributions of the present towards the future. Because this is what is at stake: the infinite narcissism of contemporary art is the mirror of the infinite narcissism of neoliberalism when everyone has forgotten that they are not alone, and that there could be a future for humanity living on earth. Art can be powerful enough to speak to, and even form the future, we have seen this in the past. However, contemporary art turns its back on the future, insisting instead on blasé, conformist novelty at worst and naughty but polite political spice at best.

DISTINCTION

Art flourishes amongst people of different classes, paths, values and different cultural, and geographic origins. But art that does not follow dominant forms, values, and origins is not considered the most "thought-provoking,"[8] is not circulated or collectable, and is thus powerless unless and until historicized, that is, co-opted. Policing images controls the imagination, thus controlling material reality. belle hooks argued this from the perspective of racism: "From slavery on, white supremacists have recognized that control over images is central to the maintenance of any system of racial domination."[9] The control over images is essential for any form of domination whether based on race, gender, class, religion, nation, sexuality and all the arbitrary locations of consigned otherness, which in neoliberalism is simply stamped on the losers of market meritocracy.

In the thick smog of the present, thinkers in research fields such as climatology, ecology, psychology, biology, medicine, agriculture, economics, and many others, are attacking the illogic of the age of kleptomania. Books have become best sellers, (on Amazon, the irony), journalism is hungry for stories about failed economic policies and inequality, and mainstream candidates for public office on both the left and the right have had to address acute symptoms of neoliberalism even though they do not agree on the root illness, seldom speak its name, define it only vaguely, and often reframe its symptoms to suit their own agendas. The myth of art and artists is strategically employed by the dominant class as evidence that their position is a fact of nature instead of a production of culture.

Art could be one of the main fields to develop other value systems and redefine vocabulary. However, we need to understand that the neoliberal project is not merely economic: it is interdisciplinary. Plehwe and Walpen summarize its strategy of diffusion: "the strength of this transnational neoliberal discourse community derives not from the highly visible and publicly acknowledged experts in politics or science and scholarship; rather, neoliberal hegemony is produced and reproduced through an expansive network that ranges across diverse institutional arenas, including academia, business, politics, and media."[10] The half-century project to normalize market society, to make its construction appear to be a natural aspect of humanity, enlists fields as wide as philosophy, law, history, sociology psychology, and of course, art. Art is a highly important piece in the portfolio of neoliberalism because of its power to imagine and reimagine society, and because artist's standpoints resonate across centuries.

DEFINING NEOLIBERALISM

Rather than rely on a vague and irresponsible familiarity of the term, we will define the concept we use throughout this book.[11] Neoliberalism is an interdisciplinary movement, developed rhetorically in reaction to war and genocide of the 20th century, aimed towards amplifying and reforming classical economic liberal policies that would supposedly strengthen individual liberty against the misery of collectivity. According to neoliberalism's founders, collective planning led to the "road to serfdom," and thus to the fascism of National Socialism and also contradictorily to communism. Personal liberty was defined in terms of liberty of property, and the method to enforce this was to legislate it via the forced competition of markets. Society would no longer be a relation between individuals and government, but of individuals with the market. Life in market society should revolve around competition, which must be enforced. Neoliberalism is a political movement used as a tool for social control.

The Mont Pèlerin Society (MPS) was named after the Swiss resort where internationally oriented, like minded, soon-to-be if not already influential people met in April 1947 with the goal of "strengthening the principles and practice of a free society." Coherence took some time to develop, but over the 2nd half of the century, the MPS developed policies for liberty of property, competition, and individualism against the collective power of socialism and unions, and these policies grew and mutated through location-specific versions into local legal codes, in nearly every country of the world.

Carried out in different stages and to differing degrees, legal implementation of neoliberalism was structured to blend in with pre-existing values and realpolitik.[12] Some nations opted for a closer reading of Hayek, reading Adam Smith, arguing that some essential services could not be handled by private business, and therefore government needed to supply them.[13] In Scandinavia and Germany for example, the ordoliberal variant blended basic worker and citizen protections along with enforced competition and privatization of certain but not all key services, overseen by a strong state. Other nations such as the United States and Chile adopted doctrines dreamed by the Chicago School of Economics forcing various brutal, anti-social, anti-democratic corporate mandates in the name of "market freedom." In China, the state-centric regime oversees free market dynamics through what anthropologist Aihwa Ong termed "graduated sovereignty and citizenship."[14] In Spain, the strong state role in ordoliberalism blended well with the bureaucratic-authoritarianism of Franco, and the paternalistic, almsgiving rule of the Catholic Church.[15]

The clever, seamless blending of neoliberal policy variants with existing structures formed patterns recognizable in many ideological shifts such as Christianity's march across local pagan traditions. Eostra was the pagan goddess of spring and her spring equinox became the root of the Easter holiday governed by the moon's phases. Related Ostara celebrations were overtaken by St. Patrick's Day. Polytheism became saints and the holy trinity arranged in celestial hierarchy. The story of a virgin birth and cyclical renewal, seen earlier in cults such as the Sybele Cult, morphed into Christmas and overwrote solstice celebrations. And like the spread of a religion, it is precisely by fusing into local myths and values that neoliberalism has seeped so deeply into the imagination within each culture. Even critics of neoliberalism use its terms and presuppositions in the same way that Satanists are still Christian: one cannot escape the mythology by operating within its cosmology. This is the fate of most art critical of the system being shown in prominent locations from within. This is also the problem of those who swear to reform the system from within: adjusting laws a few centimeters to the left or the right while remaining comfortably within its theological bounds.

Finally, neoliberalism feasts upon religion itself, colonizing with impunity: Christmas is the most important celebration of the new cosmology, cleverly rebranded with a transparent logo over the old one, welcoming even the Gods into its marketplace.

TENANT TENETS

Today's neoliberalism is the geo-political specific implementation consisting of various extremes in the legal frameworks of the following ideals:

1. Private ownership is the basis of rights and therefore trumps democracy and almost any notion of a collective public.

2. Competition is the most efficient form of economic relations, and therefore of all relations.

3. Government should exist primarily to enforce competition and to arbitrate disputes arising between private parties, but this does not mean the role of government is lesser, it means that government's primary role is to enable the market, and attack collectivity in almost all its forms.

4. Public owned and operated industries, services, and lands are inefficient, and therefore must be wholly or partially privatized, with very few exceptions.

5. The distribution of wealth flows in the direction dictated by the market, and should not be redistributed except by the whim of local almsgiving customs.

The problem with pinpointing neoliberalism in the popular consciousness is that there are so many local variations and perceived inconsistencies in practice that the term could appear to be conspiracy theory.[16] Furthermore, the stated aims of neoliberals are rarely the unspoken objectives of neoliberalism, for example, we hear the refrain of reducing government, while in practice, an authoritarian government is essential to ensure neoliberal policy is implemented and administered. Today's radical problems such as the extreme abstraction seen in financial instruments, distribution networks, free trade agreements and cryptocurrencies are too complex, except if we consider how they are weaponized tools of the system. When we look at the role of speculative finance in the collapse and misery of the losing regions and individuals of globalism, the specter of competition is always used to justify winners vs. losers in the free market.

The Mont Pèlerin Society's vision of neoliberalism could almost appear to be coordinated as a fictional conspiracy when argued as a generality.[17] The reality however, is much more complicated: while there are individuals who were and are driven to implement such policies out of an ideological, dogmatic drive, there are many, many more individuals who are only interested to game whatever system is in front of them for personal and in-group advancement (it could be neoliberalism or any other system). Neoliberal ideals are sung whenever it is self-serving to do so, and then dampened when they are not: when red states such as Florida or Texas are hit by a hurricane and their political ideologues immediately demand federal disaster compensation they forget that this is collectivism. But when disaster hits Puerto Rico, these same ideologues enforce neoliberal austerity.

It is important to understand that neoliberalism is constructed during the passage of law.[18] It is the legal implementation of the rules of the game that sets everything else in motion. In order for lawmakers to make laws, they need to give an appearance of fairness and justice. Capitalism has beat democracy[19] in part because great pains are taken to appear on the surface as though it were fair and natural. Art employed towards these ends is not neutral.

KLEPTOMANISM

For the only rational explanation why this system continues to be employed, despite the majority of humanity competing against their own best interests, we go to Adam Smith: "All for ourselves and nothing for other people, seems, in every age of the world, to have been the vile maxim of the masters of mankind."[20] What matters now is that people are stuck living in this system, and so must adjust and survive in it. Winners are well positioned as arbiters of competition, reaping massive rewards, living much larger than the kings or emperors of the past. Everyone one else is playing along because there isn't much else an individual can do when solidarity is unimaginable.

Neoliberal policies win because they suit the best interests of the few winners within it,[21] and act as a system of control for everyone else. For most, it is impossible to step outside neoliberalism, and so individuals must be well adjusted, disciplined, and continue to dream and compete for future winnings that are statistically unlikely to arrive.[22] How do these policies and laws continue to be implemented?

FICTIONAL UNIVERSES

A fictional universe is created using internal logic structures that do not correspond to fact or physics. The Star Wars Universe, for example, invented the concept of the "Force" in order to explain the telekinetic abilities of its protagonists. Intergalactic, faster-than-light-speed travel is explained by a piece of equipment called the "hyper drive" which was invented in order to narrate interplanetary relations between alien species that do not exist anywhere but in film and adolescent imagination. Almost no one attempts to seriously explain our daily life in terms of Star Wars physics. Christianity, as any religion, is also a highly detailed universe that accounts for everything from creation to after-life, believed without the burden of proof thanks to self-fulfilling, clever, hermetic logic.

Neoliberal capitalism, via its various iterations (it might be better to rename the whole thing Vile Maximism, or just Kleptomanism) is humanity's current applied fictional universe and perhaps the largest and most enveloping in the history of humanity, controlling more people than any single religion of the past. The exchange of goods and services in a marketplace seems to have been a feature aspect of human life for many thousands of years, however, the absolute monetization, gaming, and legislation of every atom within grasp has reached advanced stages of metastasis.

CORRELATIVE COSMOLOGY

Art is involved in representation, and this is exactly what is needed to implement hermetic cosmologies into daily reality. There are voluminous precedents for this process. We mention as an example the meme of building replicas of respective cosmologies expressed in frieze, pediment and niche sculptures on fantastic architecture. The Khajuraho Hindu temples in India depicted a 'world mountain' playground for gods where countless, intricately carved figures engaged in various forms of the Hindu goals of life: dharma, kama, artha and moksha. The Gigantomachy frieze from the Altar of Zeus seems to burst out of myth into life, one god even kneeling on the same stair as the viewer. The Foolish Virgins sculptures staring feverishly down from the Western Façade of the Strasbourg Cathedral dramatically demonstrated the Gospel of Matthew (25:1-13) out from church walls, down into the space of daily life. Highly detailed and improbably perched dragons and the Buddhist bodhisattva Guanyin reach fiercely down from the Longshan Temple of Manka in Taipei. Spectacular images such as these, where art imposes itself into the space of living, serve to implant conduct into the minds of masses by sensation: by naturalizing these images as though they lived and existed in the everyday.

In correlative cosmology, doctrines such as Tao served to replicate the functioning of the cosmos then infused by ritual into daily worldviews and power structures. Morality and correct action were rewarded with favor from the divine while immorality and incorrect behaviour were punished. "Heaven is humane. Heavenly rule and human rule are identical: human rule is derived from and modelled on Heaven. Human society is hierarchical. Office is rewarded on the basis of merit."[23]

Merit in the current neoliberal world is also heaven-rewarded. False truisms about competition sound so natural and well, true, that most well adjusted people can't imagine questioning their veracity. "Common sense" dictates that competition is the only way to behave, leaving all other potential behaviours unthinkable, unserious, and off the wall. All other potential systems appear to be contra to nature itself. Thus, the majority of players play the game, following the rules carefully, ensuring that neoliberalism continues until the unthinkable is no longer so.

This endless competition prevents the group labor that must be spent towards solutions, and instead actively increases inequality, exacerbates climate change, and makes everything worse for everyone, rich, poor, middle class, woman, man, gender nonconforming, cisgender, transsexual, gay, straight, bisexual, black, brown, white, faithful and the faithless. Art's role in this system is not neutral or passive.

1. Ayn Rand *The Journals of Ayn Rand*, ed. Leonard Peikoff (New York: Penguin, 1999), 36-37.

2. https://en.wikipedia.org/wiki/List_of_people_influenced_by_Ayn_Rand

3. Francis X. Rocca, "Pope Francis Says Ills of Global Economy, Not Islam, Inspire Terrorism," *Wall Street Journal* (August 1 2016).

4. Lord Jonathan Sacks, "Has Europe Lost its Soul?," *Lecture at the Pontifical Gregorian University, Rome,* December 12, 2011. https://www.unigre.it/eventi/Lord_Sacks/index_en.php. Also available here: http://rabbisacks.org/has-europe-lost-its-soul-transcript-of-lecture-delivered-at-the-pontifical-gregorian-university-rome/.

5. The Economist, "Islamic finance: Big interest, no interest," *The Economist*, September 13, 2014. https://www.economist.com/news/finance-and-economics/21617014-market-islamic-financial-products-growing-fast-big-interest-no-interest.

6. NASA, "Scientific Consensus: the Earth's Climate is Warming," https://climate.nasa.gov/scientific-consensus and American Association of the Advancement of Science, "Dear Senator...," *aaas.org*, 2009. http://www.aaas.org/sites/default/files/migrate/uploads/1021climate_letter1.pdf.

7. Catherine Wagley, "Marina Abramovic's MOCA Gala Controversy: Jeffrey Deitch Confronted and the Performers Speak Out," *LA Weekly*, December 19, 2011. http://www.laweekly.com/arts/marina-abramovics-moca-gala-controversy-jeffrey-deitch-confronted-and-the-performers-speak-out-2372380.

8. This is from the mission statement of MOMA New York, retrieved July 2016, https://www.moma.org/about.

9. bell hooks, *Black Looks. Race and Representation* (Boston: South End Press, 1992), 2.

10. Dieter Plehwe and Bernhard Walpen, *Neoliberal Hegemony: A Global Critique* (London and New York: Routledge, 2006).

11. Sentiment such as here expressed by Grewal and Purdy do not bother to locate the recorded history of the remarkably consistent policies and planned outcomes of neoliberalism, and fall into the trap set by its think tanks that purposefully obscure explicit agendas in academic diffusion. "We gladly acknowledge that neoliberalism is not conceptually neat and cannot be defined by a set of necessary and sufficient conditions for its use—a problem, if it is a problem, that neoliberalism shares with many other 'essentially contested concepts,' such as conservatism, individualism, and democracy." David Singh Grewal & Jedediah Purdy, "Introduction: Law and Neoliberalism" *Law and Contemporary Problems*, Vol 77, Number 4 (2014): 1-23.

12. A comprehensive history of the geographic specific developments of neoliberalism is developed in these books: *Mont Pèlerin The Making of the Neoliberal Thought Collective*, ed. Philip Mirowski and Dieter Plehwe (Cambridge, MA: Harvard University Press, 2009) and Aihwa Ong, *Neoliberalism as Exception: Mutations in Citizenship and Sovereignty*, (Durham and London: Duke University Press, 2006).

13. Hayek described it thusly: "To create conditions in which competition will be as effective as possible, to supplement it where it cannot be made effective, to provide the services which, in the words of Adam Smith, "though they may be in the highest degree advantageous to a great society, are, however, of such a nature, that the profit could never repay the expense to any individual or small number of individuals – These tasks provide, indeed, a wide and unquestioned field for state activity." Friedrich August Hayek, *The Road to Serfdom*, (Chicago: University Of Chicago Press, 2007), 44-45.

14. Aihwa Ong, *Neoliberalism as Exception: Mutations in Citizenship and Sovereignty*, (Durham and London: Duke University Press, 2006).

15. Historical specifics of the Spanish implementation of neoliberalism are described in detail in Cornel Ban's dissertation "Neoliberalism in Translation. Economic Ideas and Reforms in Spain and Romania," University of Maryland, 2011. http://hdl.handle.net/1903/11456.

16. Jamie Peck, *Constructions of Neoliberal Reason 1–2* (Oxford: Oxford University Press, 2010), 15. "The tangled mess that is the modern usage of neoliberalism may tell us something about the tangled mess of neoliberalism itself."

17. In case there is any doubt as to the reach of neoliberal ideologies, The Mont Pèlerin Society counts among their ranks 8 Nobel Memorial Prize in Economic Sciences winners, 1 Nobel Prize in literature, numerous professors of economics in the Ivies, and other prestigious universities around the world, and prominent elected and appointed officials in government, elected or otherwise (such as the occasion of Augustus Pinochet's brutal coup in Chile). Diffusion is and was achieved by the 485 neoliberal think-tanks in 93 countries (according to the Atlas Network). The Koch brothers fund the Cato Institute, Obamacare was an idea from The Heritage Foundation which also took a leading role during the Reagan years. The Hoover Institution is housed at Stanford University. The Rand Corporation, and the Adam Smith Institute are among the top ten most influential think tanks complied by the University of Pennsylvania. These think-tanks were established by Mont Pèlerin members such as Sir Anthony Fisher who personally founded and co-founded over 150 think tanks including IEA, and The Atlas Foundation. On the current Atlas Network website a quote attributed to British MP Oliver Letwin: "Without Fisher, no IEA; without the IEA and its clones, no Thatcher and quite possibly no Reagan; without Reagan, no Star Wars; without Star Wars, no economic collapse of the Soviet Union. Quite a chain of consequences for a chicken farmer!" Fisher himself said "Litter the world with free-market think-tanks." His grand-daughter Rachel Whetstone serves as VP of communications for Facebook, and held high positions at Uber, Google, and the British Conservative Party.

18. Such as the Supreme Court 2015 ruling Bank of America vs. Caulkett that found in favor of banks against homeowners. Or in 2016 when the Supreme Court denied an appeal on student loan erasure on bankruptcy. International trade agreements, and IMF contracts are important legal frameworks to implement neoliberal ideology, globally.

19. Martin Gilens and Benjamin I. Page, "Testing Theories of American Politics: Elites, Interest Groups, and Average Citizens," *Perspectives on Politics*, Vol 12, Issue 3, September 2014, 564-581. https://doi.org/10.1017/S1537592714001595.

20. Adam Smith, *An Inquiry Into the Nature and Causes of the Wealth of Nations* (London: T. Nelson and sons, 1884), 169.

21. Erik Sherman, "America is the richest, and most unequal, country," *Fortune Magazine*, September 30, 2015. http://fortune.com/2015/09/30/america-wealth-inequality.

22. Liz Fields, "Young People Are Poorer, Jobless, and Believe That the American Dream Is Dead", *Vice*, January 12, 2016. https://news.vice.com/article/young-people-are-poorer-jobless-and-believe-that-the-american-dream-is-dead.

23. Wm. Theodore de Bary and Irene Bloom, *Sources of Chinese Tradition*, Vol. 1 (New York: Columbia University Press, 1999), 295.

COMPETITION WINS

In neoliberalism, competition is normalized and legislated with the rhetorical position that maintaining the "efficiency of the markets" ensures the ideal "freedom of choice." Hayek framed this in the extreme terms of fulfilment versus serfdom: "Our freedom of choice in a competitive society rests on the fact that, if one person refuses to satisfy our wishes, we can turn to another. But if we face a monopolist we are at his mercy. And an authority directing the whole economic system would be the most powerful monopolist imaginable."[1] After the horrors of 20th century totalitarianism, freedom of the individual against collective planning seemed, understandably, to be paramount, and neoliberalism was thusly sold. What was left out of the sales pitch was that competition is a powerful tool used to entrench social stratification. The clear winners and losers in an economy of competition are held up as empirical evidence that the structure is natural. False scarcity is the bait, obscuring the fact that legislation enables resource corralling by kleptomaniacs.[2] In order for competition to be sold, normalized, and legislated, images are created and diffused across many fields, including art.

The hyper-competition of neoliberalism is a construction that is sold as a fact of nature, purely a matter of biology, genetics, basic psychology, and particle physics, etc. The priests, cardinals, and popes of advanced neoliberal capitalism credit all human advancements to competition.[3] We see these people in power on both the left and the right of the social spectrum, the rhetoric changing slightly to suit their audience.

Fields such as art, science, and education are antithetical to the goals of neoliberal quantification, gamification, and resulting private appropriation of everything. However, even these fields are forced to comply and compete, to great detriment of the independent goals of these fields, through coerced competition for resources via constant demands for performance metrics. For most of us it is impossible to step outside the legislated competitions of neoliberalism and so individuals must be well adjusted within the system, enabled by realist-conformist postures. Artists are no exception, and so they are forced to apply, endlessly, for grants, tenure-tracks, concourses, residencies, open calls etc., bending themselves and their work to suit norms, stabbing one another in the back, assuming any competitive edge, in the melee for attention and race horse stables. Winning or losing, competition itself is the means to normalize social psychosis, burn time, and control any opposition.

THE VILE MAXIM

Despite decades of widely recorded failures for society as a whole, (accelerating or causing increasingly extreme levels of inequality, mass food insecurity and homelessness,[4] climate change,[5] the next mass extinction of animal species,[6] the Great Pacific Garbage Patch, etc)[7] local versions of neoliberal capitalism continue to be implemented by policy makers around the world. Let's look again, now closer, at Adam Smith's formulation of the "vile maxim" to understand why:

"All for ourselves and nothing for other people, seems, in every age of the world, to have been the vile maxim of the masters of mankind. As soon, therefore, as they could find a method of consuming the whole value of their rents themselves, they had no disposition to share them with any other persons. For a pair of diamond buckles, perhaps, or for something as frivolous and useless, they exchanged the maintenance, or what is the same thing, the price of the maintenance of a thousand men for a year, and with it the whole weight and authority which it could give them. The buckles, however, were to be all their own, and no other human creature was to have any share of them; whereas in the more ancient method of expense they must have shared with at least a thousand people. With the judges that were to determine the preference this difference was perfectly decisive; and thus, for the gratification of the most childish, the meanest, and the most sordid of all vanities, they gradually bartered their whole power and authority."[8]

So, the patron saint of capitalism noted that certain humans have a tendency towards extreme greed, and that this could cause trouble for the system, and also for the winners, in the long run because they will barter their power in exchange for vanities. The vile maxim has become the primary goal in itself.[9]

What Smith could not predict is that the masters of mankind would build a system of control without hardly needing to be involved themselves, thus holding onto both power and vanity. Instead, managers, administrators, lobbyists and politicians are pay-rolled,[10] to implement legislation, normalize and reinforce their interests.[11] As a strategy, competition is enforced during almost every facet of life. Perform or perish incentives force workers, professionals and other players to perform inconsequential, ritual humiliation (via performance metrics) in order to scrape together the basics for survival, and crawl up the ranking on one's knees. Class, station, gender, race and "talent" allow players slightly more access to resources than others, however, even rank-and-file privileged must still compete amongst themselves for dwindling rewards.[12] Surplus is mostly absorbed from the highest summits via legislated, institutional, and administrative means, and this grows exponentially.

The jackpot winners of "innovative", and "disruptive" entrepreneurial wars are hailed as token examples of how well the system functions. But even in these examples, their products are quickly objects of investment by the greater masters of the universe body, controlling the few new faces in the corps.[13] Thus our masters of the universe absorb even more power and authority while appearing to merely follow the laws of the jungle.

The rhetoric of competition has been cleverly transferred to a general system of governance, and forms relations between people, and between people and their professions. In this way, competition serves both as a discourse of legitimation, and as legal framework of extreme control. It takes armies of technocrats working tirelessly, endlessly, in order to enforce the myth of competition and thus hardly "natural" in the way it is marketed. This is the important distinction of neoliberalism compared to classical liberalism: neoliberals realized the important role of government to enforce competition. The parlor trick used to disguise the active construction of competition was to transfer the metaphor of goal-oriented sports as a quantified argument for legitimation.

LEGISLATED COMPETITION IS BIG GOVERNMENT

Friedrich August von Hayek, neoliberalism's founding thinker, Mont Pèlerin Society's co-founder, "Nobel Memorial Prize in Economic Sciences"[14] winner, prescribed competition in most cases "the most efficient method we know."[15]

Hayek's formulation of "perfect competition", compared to "imperfect" or monopolistic market conditions, is the theoretical market situation where there are many sellers with homogeneous products, this information is transparent, and the seller thus cannot influence price.[16] Perfect competition is nearly impossible because the world is more complex than static, and information is unreliable. The ideal market situation for the consumer therefore is rivalry. Rivalry is when players are actively competing against each other, fighting for market share by, in theory, increasing value for the consumer, by adjusting costs, increasing innovation, and by being in tune with or resetting market preferences. Hayek wrote: "...we should worry much less about whether competition in a given case is perfect and worry much more whether there is competition at all." Thus, the only way to be sure that the market is guided by the "invisible hand" is to legislate competition with visible and enforceable laws. Legislation necessitates a strong state. To further tangle the imaginary scenario, Hayek suggested that perfect competition cannot be a goal. He wrote: "now, how many of the devices adopted in ordinary life to that end would still be open to a seller in a market in which so-called "perfect competition" prevails? I believe that the answer is exactly none."[7]

In this, and other things, Hayek and his followers were unlike 19th century liberals who advocated for laissez faire markets: neoliberalism insists on a strong state that would continuously legislate and enforce competition. Personal property will be won via competition, and legislation – via the state again – will be the guarantor of individual freedom against "tyranny." However, freedom, synonymous with success in general, must be won in the markets thus forcing everyone to compete or else. Thus the only path is infinite exploitation (especially self-exploitation) towards statistically improbable success — the only true freedom is of failure and annihilation.

It is increasingly apparent that monopoly is the planned conclusion of neoliberal policy, rendering its sales pitch pure cynicism. This point is growing clear when we are faced with the extreme monopolies seen in Amazon, Google, Comcast, Nestle, etc. These instances inspire neoliberal high priests to occasionally slap some wrists, insisting that more competition is necessary, even though these same policies led to the extreme consolidation of wealth and power in the first place. In neoliberalism, predatory domination against democratic rule (that admittedly produced the abysmal horrors of the 20th century) was precisely the plan. The circular hermeneutics of neoliberalism is becoming clear in the political economy, but we also need to look closer at how this mountebankery is also used to justify competition generally in every possible field and endeavor, even within fields where the metaphor is nonsense.

COMPETITION WINS

Let's assume for the sake of argument that competition is a sound strategy that has produced measurable results in the marketplace. Let's assume that the various near-monopolies in the United States such as too-big-to-fail banks, telecommunications, computing, heavy manufacturing etc., are anomalous in the nearly 40 years since neoliberal policies have dominated political imaginations, and the cure for the massive upward drain of resources is more competition not less. Let's assume (contradictorily), that when the competition argument is used to explain away near monopolies as winners who are winning because they offer superior products that create maximum value for the consumer, that they are acting in line with the natural inclinations of the market to reward merit. Let's continue and assume that the best, highest value products are consistently available to consumers in countries with the least regulation of the markets.[18] Let's also assume that citizens of countries where forced competition is legislated are happier, healthier, and wiser. Let's also assume here just for fun that climate change is a myth, and that it will not effect the ruling elite because the market will develop tech that allows them to breathe the air, and robots to make their espresso.

Even if all these assumptions were true, this simply does not explain the insistence of forcing competition via business and marketing strategies upon radically opposed fields where other objectives drive participation. What exactly are the objectives of science, art, education and other similar fields and how are these evaluated? It is a conceptual stretch to determine what competitive victory looks like in these fields. Rationalizing metaphors related to football or the laws of the jungle aside, is winning the golden lion at the Venice Biennial like winning the World Cup? What exactly is the effect of winning such an award other than fame? Is the art market more efficient and thus more productive for humanity because artists and scientists compete like footballers and reality TV chefs? The "art market" is not concerned with sales exclusively: the art market is the field where fame is gamed. In art as a quantified and competitive field, fame moves from the side effect to the goal in itself.

Winning is not the main motive of the doctors looking to cure cancer: however, the motive of management is to boost shareholder value and "compete" with other hospitals and eventually to overtake and buy them out. It becomes grotesque, and highly problematic to locate the "vendor", the "product", and the "consumers", in these fields, but that has become the norm in the United States. (International neoliberals are fighting to implement the U.S. style "healthcare" system on their own countries.) Education likewise moves from public good to market goods, because after all, freely available knowledge is the enemy of a competitive market, according to Hayek's above statement. The only explanation of why competition is forced upon these fields is that it is a highly efficient system to control resources, and thus to control people. The quantification of results such as testing, reputation, attention, fame, citation indices, and other ill defined and basically faith-based descriptions of "quality" in fields such as art, poetry, education, and science are the routes to "win" in these fields. The primary strategy quickly becomes to game the system itself. "Juking the Stats", and other strategies to game quantification have become the main activity, over and above any actual content or internal goals of the field itself.

THE STUPID SCIENCE

It is unproven by science to assume that the tools and methods of the forced competitive markets can simply be applied to any field, overriding the operating principles that a field may already be using. Science, for example, already has a highly functional system: it is called the scientific method and it has worked pretty well for humanity until things like patents for life-saving medicines began to pervert motives, and stymie innovation.[19] The argument for the benefits of competition is always something along the lines of "but what about all those advances, such as drugs that were developed by pharmaceutical giants mining for patents for a monopoly on the illness market?" We follow up with our own question: what about all those medicines NOT developed because they were not profitable, because of patent restrictions, because data was not shared, and because potential human capacities ended as road-kill in the competitive races to writing grants and maximizing growth? What about the potential contributions of all those minds wasting precious time filling out forms and hustling gate-keepers? The scientific method expressly and markedly relies on co-operation, coordination, peer-review based on open access to data, and the incremental improvements that come only from sharing data. Charles S. Pierce made invaluable contributions to the scientific method and humanity is better off that the title of his 1878 text published in Popular Science Monthly was not "How to Make Our Ideas Clear (to the CEO of the pharmaceutical giant, and/or interdisciplinary grant committee)."

ACADEMIC CAPITALISM

As reputation, respect and prestige are increasingly connected to success in the competitions set up to access resources, (increasingly from private foundations set up to replace public funding for science in order to "increase competitiveness") professional scientists find more of their work and careers caught up in competitive arenas. Olov Hallonsten calls this "academic capitalism" stating that: "As academic capitalism spreads, universities abandon traditional meritocratic and collegial governance to hunt money, prestige and a stronger brand."[20] In academic and professional research science, competition is seen as advantageous for the ecosystem: fighting for limited grants, research posts and teaching positions guarantee that the best come out on top, right? This faith-based belief, unfortunately, is also not backed by science. What legislated competition and competitiveness guarantees is the scientist with the most gamesmanship wins, not the scientist with the soundest science. Scientists must write catchy proposals following fickle topics using language that impresses juries of various merits. Scientists who embark on ambiguous adventures towards potentially wonderful discoveries for humanity, over the long-term, will be marginalized in the competitive science markets, public and private. If a topic is unattractive for the market of patents, grants or other immediate competitive incentives, that both corporations and corporatized universities demand, then the scientist does not get resources, and cannot devote necessary time on anything other than survival. Nobel-winner Randy Schekman on what he calls the "luxury journals" of science: "The prevailing structures of personal reputation and career advancement mean the biggest rewards often follow the flashiest work, not the best." Schekman is also critical of the competition for scientific "impact". "A paper can become highly cited because it is good science – or because it is eye-catching, provocative or wrong."[21]

Furthermore, competitive science necessitates that scientists must hide and protect their data because sharing it may assist their "competitors" (other scientists = the enemy) and cost them grants and their way up the tenure track to stability and more resources to do busy-ness science and live well in freedom. Withholding data is obviously against one of the main principles of the scientific method that has brought humankind atom shattering advancements of knowledge. Science is built on science. But neoliberal science is built on the weak foundations of competition and control.

A study by David Blumenthal and colleagues concludes: "Forty-four percent of geneticists and 32% of OLS (other life scientists) reported participating in any one of 13 forms of data withholding in the three previous years."[22] In another study, researchers Anderson, Ronning, De Vries and Martinson described the effects of competition on science as "perverse". They write: "Faced with this bleak view of the dynamics and environment of science, researchers respond with self-protective and self-promoting behaviors. If these behaviors were aligned with the progress of science and with the public trust that is embodied in public funding of research and universities, competition would prove salutary. Our findings suggest that it is not."[23]

Goodhart's Law, states that "when a measure becomes a target, it ceases to be a good measure"[24] This sums up the use of metrics across hiring, ranking, tenure, grants and other academic pursuits that become much more important than the subject studied. Peer review has been warped to be yet another form of the resource holding gate-keeper who arrive to their position by privilege and/or gaming the competition. "Ultimately, the well-intentioned use of quantitative metrics may create inequities and outcomes worse than the systems they replaced. Specifically, if rewards are disproportionally given to individuals manipulating their metrics, problems of the old subjective paradigms (e.g., old-boys' networks) may be tame by comparison."[25] The Guardian wrote about the publish or perish culture of academia: "Not long ago, Imperial College's medicine department were told that their "productivity" target for publications was to "publish three papers per annum including one in a prestigious journal with an impact factor of at least five. The effect of instructions like that is to reduce the quality of science and to demoralise the victims of this sort of mismanagement."[26]

Geneticist Mary-Claire King identified BRCA1, and thus the idea that genetics could be used as an epistemological tool.[27] Her major achievements were made despite being marginalized by the scientific establishment and the big money backers. A "child of affirmative action", as she put it herself, studied BRCA1 quietly, and "unproductively", from 1974 until her breakthrough in 1990.[28] This gigantic advance for humanity was made outside the heavy expectations of the competitive zone: she obtained modest funding, time and space from the University of Washington, a scrappy research system hanging partially intact within the ailing public university systems of the United States before it simply becomes the trade school of Microsoft/Amazon. King said "it can be liberating to not have expectations placed on you; if you can work quietly and if you can obtain funds for your work. And I could obtain modest funds for my work in the 1970s, and I could work in a way that allowed me the time and space to develop evidence until I was convinced of it."[29] This is science, it is slow, and often does not look attractive in contests.

Advancements in science are made in competition, but how many lost cures, ignored genetic markers, dismissed physical properties, and suppressed alternative energy sources are piled up in the margins of the race to oblivion? And how many potential ground breaking scientists are flushed out of the system because they don't compete well or didn't fill out the correct forms?

It is worth noting that Mary-Claire King worked in collaboration with colleagues to identify BRCA1 and is now currently collaborating with international colleagues to identify genetic causes of hearing loss and deafness. There is growing evidence of the benefits of collaboration showing that there is a correlation between the number of authors on a publication and the impact of the research. One study concluded that: "4-author publications receive more citations than other publications followed by 2-author, 3-author and single-author publication respectively."[30]Another recent study concluded that, "in general, the outcome on a given task was improved when two people worked together as opposed to individually."[31] Even the Russians and the North Americans eventually worked together in the space race leading to the International Space Station. Time scientists also cut across all geo-political and economic boundaries, as do climate scientists, and the international team at CERN.

COMPETITIVE ART

What kind of innovation occurs in the busy-ness of art dominated by hyper-competition? Goodhart's Law kicks in again here when the measure of an artist is fame. Winning grants, art awards, and stable positions (in the horse stables of galleries, and the cattle stables of art schools) are poor measures of the supposed main activity of the artist: making art. How is "winning" in the art ecosystem measured exactly? Sales? Invitations to shows? Critical discourse? Each demands fame. How does one acquire fame? A strategic yet lucky break leads to a mere-exposure bias that grows quickly into in-group bias whether on the local or globalized scenes. The whole process is normalized and everyone copes by using the just-world hypothesis and locating a phantom something or other in the art itself that must have triggered such success. Once bare-minimum thresholds are satisfied in the art ecosystem, any qualities within the work itself are secondary, unimportant for the condition of fame. The artwork may or may not be well done by any measures, because it is ultimately unimportant. Every famous artist in the last hundred years has known this, even if most couldn't admit it. This is the only explanation for the radically uneven contents of biennials, art fairs, faculty hires, etc. and for the fickle turn over of genii.

It is especially comical when the content of art turns out to be not quite how the critical market discourse has spun it: a sordid example is the ironic-appearing porcelain work containing swastikas and portraits of Hitler by Charles Krafft. A "respected figure in the Seattle art world", his collectors and cheerleaders put a veil of edgy criticality on his work while Krafft remained mute. It later turned out that Krafft was indeed a blatant white nationalist and Holocaust denier, leading one to suspect the process in Seattle of declaring someone a respected genius is suspect.[32] This kind of situation is not unique to Seattle: the demand for cheeky novelty in the art ecosystem is so ravenous, that when sober, meaningful readings of work catch up with its initial naughtiness, the work is so out of date, that criticism can be dismissed as out of date too. Innovation in a hyper-competitive busy-ness art ecosystem tends towards rapid, gestural turnover satisfying hyper-mecha-nized, market-based, cynical-cyclical structures. Cheap revolutions spinning on and on — rerum novarum cupidi, fondness for novelty. Indeterminate style change is not really innovation, it is the embodied desire to oppress by forcing everyone to be busy and to hustle towards the same dubious goal. Innovation in the hypercompetitive busy-ness of art is the same as innovation in advertising and the twenty-four hour cable news cycle: the ability to catch the attention of blasé audiences for a few seconds before they move on to the next shiny new thing to make them feel titillated for a few seconds. Attention hoarding is also a game of follow the alpha. On the battlefield of culture, those with the least to lose are the ones who gain the most: the masters of the universe orchestrate the labor of their administrators. Successfully marking market territory with trademarks, copyrights, and signature styles is not innovation: it is warfare.

Student debt disciplines artists to perform for the market, but competition controls artists absolutely. Rafael Rosendaal on his blog wrote this ironic sounding comment that is not irony. "The art world is a bit like a video game – you get to know people, you get some coins and then you get to go to the next level, and then you get into the slightly bigger room with less furniture. At first you're in the side room, then you're in the main room, then you get in the magazine, etc. The rules are very set, you talk to this person, a biennale, then you get a gold star, then you get upgraded and get to speak to better curators – but then also the critics are harsher... So really, it's just like Super Mario."[33] It is fully understandable for a realist-conformist artist to compete as though life were a video game, to please uncritically in order to get the gold star. However understandable, this stance comes only from weakness: do not dare to dream anything beyond your immediate bonds and the temporary satiation of consumption.

Although freedom is promised, such realism-conformism works primarily for the benefit of the top of the hierarchy because it keeps everyone running through programmed obstacle courses. The busy-ness of art demands market-based solutions to soul-based problems. Artists must compete amongst themselves for choked resources in ever-tighter cycles in one of the most competitive fields of them all. In this way, contemporary art is the model for the neoliberal, winner-take-all, entrepreneurial battlefield. Administrators gleefully play their roles, enforcing competition by running interminable concourses. Art managers squeeze as much value as possible while minimizing expenditure and risk. Artists feebly allow someone else to set their goals for them, and are left to win petty gold stars floating aimlessly in the deep expanse of contemporary desolation.

ART PRIZES AND WAGES

Let's have a look at several local and world-class examples of con-courses of art and the prize monies associated with them:

London: The Turner Prize: £ 40,000
New York, The Hugo Boss award: $100,000
New York, Bucksbaum Award: $100,000
Grand Rapids, Mi: The Artprize: top prize is $200,000
Paris, Duchamp Prize: €35,000
Kiev, Future Generations Art Prize: $100,000
Seattle, Neddy Artist Awards: $25,000
Detroit, Kresge Artist Fellows: $25,000
Oslo, Statoil Art Award: NOK 500,000 (approx. $65,000)

With each of these prizes, one person gets the equivalent of a yearly income of a working class, middleclass, or in a few cases, upper-middle class employee salary. The prize money is enough to live on for a while, especially if the artist is thrifty and lives in a cheap city. However, these prizes are given to an artist only once in their lifetimes, and it is rare for an artist to win more than one or two of these kinds of prizes. Thus, art prizes are not equivalent to a basic living wage for an artist who by the industry's measurements is a great artist, and/or a "genius." Further absurdity is added in the cases of the larger prizes, where the winners are almost always already famous, and long gone are the years of struggle when they could have actually really used the money.

The smaller prizes like in Detroit and Seattle are table scraps from the plutocracy that somehow encourage local artists to fight like wild dogs amongst themselves. In each case, large or small, the real winner of the prize is the giver of the prize gaining the most in terms of advertising, white-washing, tax deduction vortexes, and outright insider trading when they collect and resale the same artists they give awards to.

Some prizes do not even award money, offering nothing but the promise of "exposure." For example the four artists nominated in 2017 for Germany's top contest, Preis der Nationalgalerie, which counts on BMW as its main sponsor, denounced that the prize showed a "self-congratulatory use of diversity," the prize's ceremony "seemed to be more of a celebration of the sponsors and institutions than a moment to engage with the artists and their works."[34]

Symbolically, these prizes serve to establish the masters-of-the-universe as the powerful arbiters of what is good and bad in the universe. Practically, these prizes realize an important mandate to legislate competition in this and every possible field and aspect of life. What we would like to see instead is a yearly 1 million dollar prize for the fastest artist in a one hundred meter dash. We would call it the Speedy Genius Award. It would be funny to see artists training vigorously with running coaches, eyeing each other belligerently from across the running tracks of Williamsburg and Kreuzberg. This prize would have a clear rubric, and a clear winner without room for interpretation, extrapolation or bias. Sponsors could stipulate that artists must compete with Mickey Mouse ears and Ronald McDonald shoes.

For most artists, the promise of future concretized capital lands as often as a lottery win. A lottery is the structure that most resembles material success in art, and that is the point. Artists and other cultural workers must contribute endless time and mental energy to busy-ness, throwing lives into the black hole of culture, in the vague hope that their sacrifices will fit into the bigger framed picture, and meanwhile praying that some meagre resources return for basic survival. Neoliberal conformist-realists will scoff that these people should get another job because the market has spoken.

Of course, forced competition is about controlling anyone who could use their time or talents towards threats to order such as social critique and alternative visions for better living. Forced competition is about controlling the populace and ultimately preventing collective action or democratic governance. Artists, like all other professions in our age of kleptomania, are fed the dogma of competition as though solidarity and collaboration were not even an option. However, unlike other professions where there are at least minimum wages, the vast majority of artists win nothing in return for their labor, and therefore only lottery winners and children of oligarchs can choose to be artists without sacrificing their lives.

PSEUDO-COLLABORATION

Even collaboration is packaged, marketed, and sold competitively. The most cynical of all the examples of pseudo collaboration we can offer in art is the so-called "social practice" and "relational aesthetics" movements that aestheticizes and co-opts cooperation itself. The norm is for social practice and relational aesthetics "stars" to enter a "community" and engage mostly struggling groups of people, including other artists, by a commission from a local tax-exempt art ecosystem. The practice cynically takes up social obligations that neoliberal government has left behind such as for education, mental health, and social work, effectively privatising them to reflect the anti-democratic whims of the members of the local art ecosystem. Since these works usually involve uncompensated or undercompensated labor, bodies are used as material, and the resulting work is called "collaboration" even though the artist is unfailingly credited with authorship. Unnamed bodies and their labour are managed and directed by the artist, who wields power, absorbs the social capital, and is the highest paid "collaborator" in a purposefully skewed social relation. The social practice and relational aesthetics artist manages masses of bodies in order to advance the branding interests of themselves as a corporation, and their corporate shareholders which includes actual corporate sponsors, the museums and their boards, galleries and collectors, university programs and other players in the contemporary art ecosystem, which is in the neoliberal ecosystem. We remind the reader of the grotesque spectacle of thousands of wreathing bodies during the ceremonies of the Beijing Olympics, which could also fit under the terms "social practice".

Since collectivity is considered the "road to serfdom", what a fitting end to also figure out how to privatise all forms of it.

CORPORATE COOPERATION

Another kind of related pseudo-collaboration is corporate collaboration. When cooperation manifests as competitive team sports, this is the neoliberal ideal. Corporate cooperation emphasizes team-building through conformity, constraint and blind ambition within an oppressive, military hierarchy that actively works against democracy. Corporate cooperation is post individualism fully implemented into a military structure where individuals in fact no longer have value, even the CEO is expelled when necessary. Nearly every element in the corporation is interchangeable, this is its resilient power. The goal in the ranks is to advance to the top where the individual is finally able to enforce freewill, but this is illusion since the corporate body itself employs antibodies at the slightest sign of infection.

HYPERCOMPETITION

The term hypercompetition perhaps originates from psychoanalyst Karen Horney in her theories on neurosis. She identified a highly aggressive personality type who needs to compete and win at any cost as a means of maintaining their self-worth. According to Horney, these individuals are likely to turn any activity into a competition, and feel threatened if they find themselves losing, even if the stakes are imaginary and the entire act is harmful to everyone.

Hypercompetition is implemented fairly easily because it appeals to the ego and self-worth of people, and it sounds logical in principal to compete with others for things that you want, and this is how it is sold, as the law of the jungle. What is rarely considered is that hypercompetition burns energy and time, thus preventing resistance, ensuring the efficiency of the militarized social hierarchy.

Our options are few: drop out and starve, or stay in and brawl with the bruisers and with each other, thus making us all brutes. The predatory nature of advanced neoliberal capitalism makes us atomized enemies of one another. We must compete for basic resources that are owned and administered by fewer and fewer.

"Hypercompetition is a state in which the rate of change in the competitive rules of the game are in such flux that only the most adaptive, fleet, and nimble... will survive."[35] What does this mean, fleet and nimble? It means the ability to adapt, quickly and be well-adjusted, simulating thinking. This appears to be freedom of movement, but in fact, it is the opposite: one must follow the brawl in lockstep. For example, every high-tech invention is followed by immense and brutal waves of litigation, and it is in the courts where the survival of "innovation" is determined whether or not the invention is beneficial. To be nimble in the market means to follow trends as fast as possible, by switching off the brain to allow instinct to be manipulated straight off the approaching cliff.

THE MUSIC INDUSTRY

Alan Krueger, the Chairman of President Obama's Council of Economic Advisers (not exactly a wild radical) noted that luck has more to do with success than talent. Talent should be found out by competition, which naturally favours the talented — isn't that right? We reproduce a big chunk of the text here as it shows growing mainstream recognition of our psychotic moment in time, even from within neoliberal administrations themselves.

"The music industry is a microcosm of what is happening in the U.S. economy at large. We are increasingly becoming a "winner-take-all economy," a phenomenon that the music industry has long experienced. Over recent decades, technological change, globalization and an erosion of the institutions and practices that support shared prosperity in the U.S. have put the middle class under increasing stress. The lucky and the talented – and it is often hard to tell the difference – have been doing better and better, while the vast majority has struggled to keep up. These same forces are affecting the music industry. Indeed, the music industry is an extreme example of a "super star economy," in which a small number of artists take home the lion's share of income. Let me next turn to the role of luck. I said "best artists," but I also could have added luckiest artists. Luck plays a major role in the rock 'n roll industry. Success is hard to judge ahead of time, and definitely not guaranteed, even for the best performers. Tastes are fickle, and herd behavior often takes over."[36]

FIGHTING FREEDOM

The hypercompetitive vocabulary of the high tech sector crosses easily into the busy-ness of art (and education) where administrators accept it eagerly. Business vocabulary and strategies win in the short term. Business and high tech operatives cannot afford to think, to reflect, to take stock, ponder, or to move freely. If they do any of these things, they will be completely ravaged by competitors who will take advantage of even the slightest pause in busy-body activity. This activity is all very exciting, and also very stupid, in that it pushes short-term action, reward and "winning" as its primary value.

Art adopts business vocabulary because it appears to be a quantifiable way to judge art and artists. The ambiguity of the goals, rubrics, purposes and achievements of art is unbearable to most people, even within the art world. This priceless quote from Blouin demonstrates: "Auerbach favors minimalist garments of bright, often monochrome hues, and tassel-and-rope-festooned accessories, all of which complement her artworks quite nicely when she poses in front of them. She can often be spotted wearing wonderful bright yellow desert boots, which are clearly made for walking — all over the competition."[37]

The only results of this kind of competition is the entropic dumping of plastic into the oceans, and energy into time and cold, deep space: the endless, mindless spinning of business-as-usual that has caused the global warming that is accelerating beyond predictions: even the level-headed Director of Godard Space Studies at NASA simply said "Wow."[38]

Many artists turned originally to art because it has an image of freedom. Freedom is an abstract concept, but let's imagine what that could mean: an artist is free to explore, free to break mores, free to dismiss convention, free to think and state inconvenient thoughts, free to avoid the competitive sports that violently unify goals. And perhaps most of all, the artist is supposedly free to organize their time. These myths, of course, are simply not what most artists find in reality.

AGENCY COOPERATION

Agency Cooperation is the powerful opposite of neoliberal competition and corporate cooperation. Agency Cooperation is the active refusal to be oppressed, and, crucially, the refusal to oppress in return, in the present or future. To strive for liberation and resist all oppression, as in Paulo Freire's observation: "The oppressed, instead of striving for liberation, tend themselves to become oppressors."[39]

Agency Cooperation is the vehicle instead of the mythical end state. Agency Cooperation is as powerful as water when enough molecules join together.

THE ART OF FREE TIME

We would like to consider a simple, holistic strategy. There should be no professional artists at all. All art should be produced by amateurs with heart, unmoved by competition or prizes, same with musicians. Burst inflated winnings, inflated jobs and positions, and inflated declarations of genius. How could this be accomplished? Re-build the economy, and the role of collective government, starting with some form of the redistribution of resources, and leave everyone with tremendous free time. Even conservative John Meynard Keynes predicted that production and living standards in many countries would be high enough to allow a 15 hour work week, delivering everyone riches of free time. (He did not predict how strong the vile maxim would become.) Imagine the things people could imagine with time, without the fear and stress of precarity. ("Poor folk anxiety" is how artist Sondra Perry calls this condition,[40] spreading into almost all classes.) Some people would drag or become opiate addicts, but the great majority would invest their lifetimes in interests that could improve the world, or at least make it gentler and more fun. Scientists would devote their time and faculties towards unforeseen benefits rather than grant applications. Everyone would become a chef, a gardener, a baker or a brewer.

Only after an economic system is functioning for the majority, and dignity is no longer rare and precious like diamonds, (dignity should be common like air), then everyone could develop who knows what wild ideas (some terrible, some wonderful) in the ample free time available to everyone. Art spaces could pop up everywhere like parks, or within other public spaces. Science labs, sculpture studios, and wood shops could be located in every neighbourhood, maintained by trained individuals who would put in their 15 hours a week there, (or maybe only 8 by then), and spend their free time somewhere else. Everyone would be driven by the natural curiosity that would bloom forth from the rock it had been smashed under in neoliberal capitalism. Social life after post-precarity, and post-scarcity would be completely unrecognizable to us now. (Even imaginary post-scarcity Star Trek was based on a military organization of people concerned mostly with fighting other species at their borders.) Only after a post-scarcity and post-precarity organization of life would the widest possible range of voices, viewpoints and contributions come from everywhere, expanding human society equally, making life more fun and self-actualized than in the stunted, brutal, waking nightmare of neoliberal capitalism. "Community" would be defined as people working together towards a wide array of mutually beneficial goals instead of the hawkish, selfish, special economic interest groups the word implies now.

Divide and conquer is not inevitable. Competition is sold like the inevitable, natural state of an advanced society. Competition is the most efficient system to feed the "Vile Maxim" and cooperation is the most efficient system to feed people.

1. F.A. Hayek, "The Road to Serfdom," *Condensed Version, Reader's Digest* (1945): 63.

2. Deborah Hardoon, Sophia Ayele and Ricardo Fuentes-Nieva, "An Economy for the 1%," OXFAM, January 18, 2016. https://www.oxfam.org/en/pressroom/pressreleases/2016-01-18/62-people-own-same-half-world-reveals-oxfam-davos-report.

3. Straw-man or meme? Paul Romer, the chief economist of the World Bank in an interview: "Q: Is it correct to say that the goal of a Charter City is to encourage competition among cities? Romer: Almost. I would say the goal is to improve the quality of governance, and that competition and startups are one means of achieving this goal." https://paulromer.net/tag/charter-cities/ Furthermore, Reuters reported French president Emmanuel Macron stating that France must be a country that "thinks and moves like a start up... because your competitors do not wait." http://www.reuters.com/article/us-france-tech-macron-idUSKBN1962L3. Here is another example among millions, competition, according to Shaun Rosenberg: "Advances The Human Civilization. If there was no competition we would have never landed on the moon". http://www.shaunrosenberg.com/10-reasons-why-competition-is-a-good-thing. And here is another one: http://businessgross.com/2013/01/21/business-competition/

4. The U.S. Conference of Mayors' Report on Hunger and Homelessness, 2016. https://endhomelessness.atavist.com/mayorsreport2016.

5. Adrian Parr, *The Wrath of Capital. Neoliberalism and Climate Change Politics* (New York: Columbia University Press, 2012).

6. Gerardo Ceballos, Paul R. Ehrlich, Anthony D. Barnosky, Andrés García, Robert M. Pringle and Todd M. Palmer, "Accelerated modern human–induced species losses: Entering the sixth mass extinction," *Science Advances* (05 June 2015). http://advances.sciencemag.org/content/1/5/e1400253.

7. Rockström, J., Schellnhuber, H. J., Hoskins, B., Ramanathan, V., Schlosser, P., Brasseur, G. P., Gaffney, O., Nobre, C., Meinshausen, M., Rogelj, J. and Lucht, W. "The world's biggest gamble," *Earth's Future*, 4, (2016): 465–470. doi:10.1002/2016EF000392. Also see the text "Art in the Age of Kleptomania" in this book.

8. Adam Smith, *An Inquiry Into the Nature and Causes of the Wealth of Nations* (London: T. Nelson and sons, 1884), 169.

9. Gerry Mullany, "World's 8 Richest Have as Much Wealth as Bottom Half, Oxfam Says" *New York Times* (January 16, 2017).

10. Wikipedia, "Citizens United," https://en.wikipedia.org/wiki/Citizens_United_(organization).

11. This text was written before Trump was elected president of the US. Our formulation stands: it is not the first time a plutocrat is used as a tool for other plutocrats, see George W. Bush, Putin, Bloomberg, and the whole cast of sordid characters running Saudi Arabia.

12. Nathan Joo and Richard V. Reeves, "Not just the 1%: Upper middle class income separation," *Brookings Institution*, September 10, 2015. https://www.brookings.edu/blog/social-mobility-memos/2015/09/10/not-just-the-1-upper-middle-class-income-separation.

13. Facebook Inc. shareholders. https://finance.yahoo.com/quote/FB/holders?p=FB.

14. Nobel Memorial Prize in Economic Sciences was invented in order to normalize Economics as a science in the imagination of the public, the neoliberal think-tank Mont Pelerin Society count 8 winners among their members, since the invention of the prize in 1968.

15. Friedrich A. Hayek, "The Meaning of Competition," *Mises Institute*, excerpt from a Princeton University lecture from May 20, 1946. https://mises.org/library/meaning-competition.

16. Imperfect market conditions seem to be the natural end neoliberal policies, despite the rhetorics, clearly reserving "freedom" for the oligarchy.

17. Friedrich A. Hayek, *Individualism and Economic Order* (Chicago: University of Chicago Press, 1948), 96.

18. Claire Cain Miller, "Why the U.S. Has Fallen Behind in Internet Speed and Affordability," *New York Times*, October 30, 2014. https://www.nytimes.com/2014/10/31/upshot/why-the-us-has-fallen-behind-in-internet-speed-and-affordability.html.

19. Gold, Kaplan, Orbinski, Harland-Logan and N-Marandi, "Are Patents Impeding Medical Care and Innovation?," *Plos Medicine Journal* (2010). https://doi.org/10.1371/journal.pmed.1000208.

20. Olov Hallonsten, "Corporate Culture Has No Place in Academia", *Nature Magazine*, Issue 538 (October 3, 2016). doi: doi.org/10.1038/538007a. http://www.nature.com/news/corporate-culture-has-no-place-in-academia-1.20724

21. Randy Shenkman, "How Journals like Nature, Cell, and Science are Damaging Science," *The Guardian*, December 9, 2013. http://www.theguardian.com/commentisfree/2013/dec/09/how-journals-nature-science-cell-damage-science.

22. Blumenthal, D., Campbell, E. G., Gokhale, M., Yucel, R., Clarridge, B., Hilgartner, S., & Holtzman, N. A. "Data withholding in genetics and other life sciences: Prevalences and predictors," *Academic Medicine*, 81 (2006): 137–145.

23. Melissa S. Anderson, Emily A. Ronning Raymond De Vries Brian C. Martinson, "The Perverse Effects of Competition on Scientists' Work and Relationships," *Springer Science, Business Media B.V.* November 21, 2007. https://doi.org/10.1007/s11948-007-9042-5.

24. Lewis Elton "Goodhart's law and performance indicators in higher education," *Evaluation and Research in Education*, Vol. 18, (2004): 120. https://doi.org/10.1080/09500790408668312

25. Edwards Marc A. and Roy Siddhartha, "Academic Research in the 21st Century: Maintaining Scientific Integrity in a Climate of Perverse Incentives and Hypercompetition" *Environmental Engineering Science*, Volume: 34 Issue 1 (January 2017): 51-61. https://doi.org/10.1089/ees.2016.0223.

26. David Colquhoun, "Publish-or-perish: Peer review and the corruption of science," *The Guardian*, September 5, 2011. https://www.theguardian.com/science/2011/sep/05/publish-perish-peer-review-science.

27. Mary-Claire King, "'The Race' to Clone BRCA1", *Science*, Vol. 343, Issue 6178, (March 28, 2014): 1462-1465.

28. King, "'The Race' to Clone BRCA1"

29. Ibid.

30. Alireza Abbasi, Liaquat Hossain, and Christine Owen, "Exploring the relationship between research impact and collaborations for Information Science," *System Science* (HICSS), (2012), doi: 10.1109/HICSS.2012.664.

31. Bahador Bahrami, Karsten Olsen, Peter E. Latham, Andreas Roepstorff, Geraint Rees, Chris D. Frith, "Optimally Interacting Minds," *Science,* Vol. 329, Issue 5995 (August 27, 2010): 1081-1085. doi: 10.1126/science.1185718.

32. Rachel Arens, "Charles Krafft and the Conundrum of Nazi Art," *The New Yorker*, March 23, 2013. "http://www.newyorker.com/culture/culture-desk/charles-krafft-and-the-conundrum-of-nazi-art.

33. Interview with Rafael Rozendaal, "Abstract Browsing," *Dis Magazine*, 2013. http://dismagazine.com/discussion/73124/rafael-rozendaal-abstract-browsing.

34. Benjamin Sutton "Nominees Denounce Germany's Biggest Art Prize," *Hyperallergic*, November 10, 2017. https://hyperallergic.com/411044/nominees-denounce-germanys-biggest-art-prize.

35. Bizshifts-Trends, "Facing Challenge of HyperCompetition– Fast, Smart, Bold: Traditional Competitive Strategies are Not Sustainable...," *Bizshifts-Trends*, June 9, 2006. http://bizshifts-trends. com/2012/09/06/facing-the-challenge-of-hypercompetition-faster-smarter-bolder-traditional-strategies-are-not-sustainable.

36. Alan B. Krueger, "Land of Hope and Dreams: Rock and Roll, Economics and Rebuilding the Middle Class," *Remarks prepared for the Rock and Roll Hall of Fame*, Cleveland, June 12, 2013. https:// obamawhitehouse.archives.gov/sites/ default/files/docs/hope_and_dreams_-_ final.pdf.

37. Submitted by admin, *Blouin Art Info*, October 22, 2010. http://www. blouinartinfo.com/node/104574.

38. https://twitter.com/ClimateOfGavin/ status/708701233763188737

39. Paulo Freire, *Pedagogy of the Oppressed* (New York: Herder and Herder, 1970)

40. Sondra Perry and Nicole Maloof, "C.R.E.A.M.," in *Forms of Education: Couldn't Get a Sense of It* (Seattle: INCA Press, 2016), 393.

FREEDOM

Everyone, it seems, is in favor of freedom.[1] Liberty meant no more than freedom from unjustified restraint, and as such was fundamentally identical with freedom of movement.[2] It is action, not rest, that constitutes our pleasure.[3] Radical freedom and love; radical love and freedom.[4] The aim of sadism is to transform a man into a thing, something animate into something inanimate, since by complete and absolute control the living loses one essential quality of life - freedom.[5] The day that the black man takes an uncompromising step and realizes that he's within his rights, when his own freedom is being jeopardized, to use any means necessary to bring about his freedom or put a halt to that injustice, I don't think he'll be by himself.[6] In that field of possibility we have the opportunity to labour for freedom, to demand of ourselves and our comrades, an openness of mind and heart that allows us to face reality even as we collectively imagine ways to move beyond boundaries, to transgress. This is education as the practice of freedom.[7] This educational work is not really the pedagogy of the oppressed, it is indeed the pedagogy of the liberated, because if you do not have training in the practice of freedom, when you win... it will not last.[8] Dehumanization dehumanizes the dehumanizers as much as the dehumanized.[9] The difficulty of finding genuine and disinterested support for a systematic policy for freedom is not new.[10] Sadistic love is a perverted love – a love of death, not of life. One of the characteristics of the oppressor consciousness and its necrophilic view of the world is thus sadism. As the oppressor consciousness, in order to dominate, tries to deter the drive to search, the restlessness, and the creative power which characterize life, it kills life.[11] If you don't have food you can't be free.[12] To he whose tanks crush all the roses in the garden. Who breaks windows in the night. Who sets fire to a garden and museum and sings of freedom.[13] We know through painful experience that freedom is never voluntarily given by the oppressor, it must be demanded by the oppressed.[14] Intellectual freedom cannot exist without political freedom; political freedom cannot exist without economic freedom; a free mind and a free market are corollaries.[15] The more widespread their mastery of the world, the more they find themselves crushed by uncontrollable forces.[16] Economic freedom is an end in itself to a believer in freedom. In the second place, economic freedom is also an indispensable means toward the achievement of political freedom.[17] But intellectual work, broadly defined, matters, and rather than angrily dismiss its value, we might consider instead thinking and rethinking its place in the world, and working to make a case that the essential values we claim to hold dear, including those that what we term "democracy" and "freedom," owe everything to including a spirit of intellectual inquiry that embraces instead of rejecting abstractions, thoughts, and lines of query that might, eventually go nowhere in terms of published work but whose formation in themselves are the driving engine of what we might term public life itself.[18] If art's function is to articulate a notion of human freedom then the problem is how to make the notion of freedom relevant to everybody, not just an élite group.[19] And I've been interested in freedom practically all my life.[20] Without general elections, without freedom of the press, freedom of speech, freedom of assembly, without the free battle of opinions, life in every public institution withers away, becomes a caricature of itself, and bureaucracy rises as the only deciding factor.[21]

1. John Hospers
2. Hannah Arendt
3. John Adams
4. Cornel West
5. Erich Fromn
6. Malcolm X
7. bell hooks
8. Gayatri Spivak
9. Jean-Paul Sartre
10. Friedrich A. Hayek
11. Paulo Freire
12. Grace Lee Boggs
13. Samih Al-Qasim
14. Martin Luther King Jr.
15. Ayn Rand
16. Simone de Beauvoir
17. Milton Friedman
18. Yasmin Nair
19. Mierle Laderman Ukeles
20. Angela Davis
21. Rosa Luxemburg

WEIRD ART

WEIRD people (White, Educated, Institutional, Rich, Democrat-leaning)*[1] dominate the art ecosystem. One of the many tools at their disposal is taste. Through science-sounding but thinly formed discourses, the word taste is seldom used explicitly, (that would be bad taste), but it is implied through many forms.

The WEIRD art ecosystem is yet another location where fiction is normalized. Let's have a look at how taste and related claims of universality are implicit strategies.

It is often claimed in the discourse circles of the art ecosystem such as art schools, press, and trade publications that there are universal aspects of formal art.[2] This idea is old, but became popular at least with Documenta II in 1959,[3] corresponding exactly with the apex of high modernism. The argument goes something like this: those with taste are able to discern the forms, shapes, colors, tones, and patterns that make up a superior, formally successful work of art. Such a successful work of art can be recognized universally as such. Those who disagree are uncultured, ignorant to the rules of formalism, and are simply not able to recognize art's transcendence. How this is accomplished is by conflating works of art with other more "rational" systems such as mathematics, geometry, and physics whose veracity is unassailable. For example, the "musicality" of abstract and formal works is tied into claims of mathematical formula. Mathematic truth cannot be disputed, and is thus universal, recognizable by even aliens. NASA wrote about the record included in the Voyager deep space probe "Using the universal language of science and math, they also found ways to communicate our location in the galaxy and how long ago the spacecraft was launched."[4]

Equating hypothetical aliens of Alpha Centauri with the aliens of actual Peru is a far too common practice among European descendants. Furthermore, the "universality" of mathematics is an interesting assumption considering the very cultural, language and visual specific uses of the symbols of mathematics such as + - # < > % =, etc. And finally, the tenuous connection between the "musicality" of visual compositions and the universal language of music unravels quickly: we only need to consider the wide range of different types of musical scales using completely different mathematical intervals such as the Persian, Indonesian, Hejaz, Yo, Ionian, Hirajoshi, Gamalan, Raga systems, and other systems utilizing drones, glissando, screams, atonality, or arrhythmic arrangements.

Authoritative language can be employed towards whatever fictions necessary to reproduce power. Scientific racism, for example, is an earnest practice, and it is alive and well in US and EU police and refugee policies, in sports theories, and other race-biology fictions.[5]

However, unlike scientific racism, assumptions, declarations, and assertions of "good" and "universal" taste in art and art criticism (and other marketplaces of art) are hardly backed up with even empirical sounding evidence, let alone actual empirical research. Comparisons and equivalences form the gesticular crux for connoisseurs working the bullet-proof standards of taste in a room. When examples are given, they come in the form of the colonial-colonized narrative where the "savage" learns the "right" way of doing things from the "civilizer", and thus the "savage" learns to appreciate the "universal" nature of a Picasso, or a Beethoven, while simultaneously describing how these heroes have distilled the primitive influence into civilized form.

Though mainstream in sociology at least since Pierre Bourdieu's 1979 book *Distinction*, the hegemonic understanding of taste has not penetrated the art ecosystem except to turn the word taste distasteful. Art's apologists simply disregard the word as a relic of another time while riding its premises without change. This is the same mechanism as the centrist racist's insistence of living in a "post race" world where racism is somehow a relic of another time.

A related study on taste was done by the Russian artist duo Komar & Melamid as an artwork called "The Most Wanted Paintings".[6] Based on random sample surveys (1001 people in the USA) they discovered what was the most wanted and unwanted painting in each surveyed country. Neither the "wanted" nor the "unwanted" paintings would be hot collectors items in any western museum board member's stately homes. The least wanted painting among the majority of nations surveyed was an abstract, modern looking thing. Art professionals, and the artists themselves might have a laugh that democratic selection of art is simply not possible, because the public is simply too ignorant to be trusted with aesthetics. The mystery invoked here is that if formalism were a "universal" language then why did the masses surveyed among 14 countries of Europe, Asia, Africa and North America not understand this and select abstract painting as their preferred art? Is good taste universal, or must it be learned? The double bind tightens.

In the study "Abstract Art as a Universal Language" Brinkmann, et al, studied eye movements of subjects looking at abstract paintings by Kandinsky, Pollock and Motherwell (all works shown in Documenta II, the "universal" one). They found that art historians shared similar analysis patterns with each other, as with artists, but people from other professions fixated on heterogeneous areas of the paintings. The only formal aspect among the paintings that drew most subjects were bright colors and shapes that resembled human faces. The conclusion to their study stated that "eye-movement patterns clearly were more heterogeneous for abstract compared to representational art."[7] At least two related New York Times articles, one titled "Can Taste Be Taught?",[8] and the other "Is Good Taste Teachable?",[9] run with the assumption is that this question is novel, especially to the art historian who, condescendingly, and "fervently contends that you can".

Deniz Tekiner wrote about the connection of taste to the market. "By its judgments of taste, formalist criticism certified the worthiness of art objects for markets, facilitating processes of the reception of artworks as commodities. It thus functioned symbiotically with art marketers."[10] His focus was on Clement Greenburg's taste in modern art, but this is not the first suggestion that art is connected to the marketplace. The consistent link is that certain taste-making customers are always right. Pushing past the days of relativism, today's globalized art ecosystem of novelty and information-driven eclecticism never admits failure. Museum directors, gallery owners, collectors, art professors, juries for awards and grants, and all the other standard bodies of selection and exclusion never lose confidence in their own powers of superior distinction. Not one jury during relativism or afterwards declared that they simply didn't know how to proceed when tasked with distinguishing the winners from the losers. The athletic avoidance of concrete language avoids detection and demonstrates that their taste is anything but objective. Instead what they say is something like "outstanding exhibition,"[11] and never explain what that means. What is rarely acknowledged or declared is that the ability to determine an "outstanding contribution" stems from the same place as taste: a symptom of belonging to a very particular group.

A blow against psychology also knocks into aesthetics: methodology turns out to be determinant. In his book "The Weirdest

People in the World" Joseph Henrich writes that "Behavioral scientists routinely publish broad claims about human psychology and behavior in the world's top journals based on samples drawn entirely from Western, Educated, Industrialized, Rich, and Democratic (WEIRD) societies. Researchers – often implicitly – assume that either there is little variation across human populations, or that these "standard subjects" are as representative of the species as any other population." He spent years doing field studies in Peru, New Guinea and other extra-euro civilizations systematically reproducing standard psychological experiments with much wider groups of people than originally included for study. Since 96% of psychological samples come from countries with only 12% of the world's population, it made sense to expand sample sizes deeper into the world. It is not surprising that Henrich recorded wild variations across different cultures around the world, upending what were previously considered universal human psychological traits and behaviors.

Universal assumptions within branches of psychology, economics, behavioral sciences, and we add, art, are norms across much of the world's most powerful institutions. Unqualified human traits are, of course, the norms of any particular hegemonic group that are forcibly applied to other groups. One does not even need to leave one's country to find groups with different traits and behaviors: by simply exploring different immigration statuses, genders, races, sexual orientations, classes, and national backgrounds, one finds distinction. What is clear is that "universal" claims record and justify local dominant world-beliefs (belief as opposed to facts) that are then implemented with institutional violence such as racism, xenophobia, sexism and classism. When institutions claim that they are interested in "preserving, and documenting a collection of the highest order"[12] and "world-class"[13] art, it is a WEIRD declaration.

*

We of course took the main subject for this text from Joseph Henrich's text, but we here re-work the thesis to apply to the art ecosystem.

White:
in order for a person of color to be admitted, they must adapt to dominant WEIRD standards, or wait to be co-opted.

Educated:
and furthermore, educated by the most elite institutions.

Institutional:
management of art is more important than art and artists.

Rich:
either rich or loyal to and hoping to join the rich.

Democrat-leaning:
liberal rhetorical positions do not actually mean democratic.

1. Henrich, J., Heine, S. J., & Norenzayan, A., "The weirdest people in the world?," *Behavioral and Brain Sciences*, 33 (2-3) (2010): 61-83.

2. Straw man or meme?
– John M. Eger, "Art Is a Universal Language," *Huffington Post*, February 24, 2015. https://www.huffingtonpost.com/john-m-eger/if-art-is-a-universal-lan_b_806787.html.
"Maybe it is naive to say art is the universal language, and that we c an open windows for all to see that we are just folks, and that we are one community. Yet, if art can't, nothing can."
– Cherie Z. Hu, "The Universal Language of Art," *The Harvard Crimson*, April 9, 2015. http://www.thecrimson.com/column/artistic-matchmaker/article/2015/4/9/artist-matchmaker-universal-language.
"In these projects, although participants come from diverse cultural backgrounds with different means, standards, and gestures of communication, art becomes a powerful unifying force, serving as the common language that all involved can speak."
– Goethe-Institute, 2016, Fikrun Wa Fann in an interview with Heinz Mack: "Oriental art as a whole has one feature in common: it has no object." (??!!) And "Art is a universal language. It used to relate only to the West – now it is opening up towards the East."
– On a syllabus for the class *Formalism (also known as New Criticism)* at Armstrong Atlantic State University:
"The major premises of New Criticism include: "art for art's sake," "content = form," and "texts exist in and for themselves." Along the way, New Criticism wants to pull out and discuss any universal truths that literary works might hold concerning the human condition."
– Ken Johnson, "Reading With One Eye Closed," *Art in America*, March 30, 2013. http://www.artinamericamagazine.com/news-features/magazines/reading-with-one-eye-closed.
"Among elite dealers and collectors, identity-based art is less valued. The dominant demographic in that realm has a solidarity of its own, though it ordinarily does not call attention to itself. The high-end art world would like us to believe that it adheres to transcendent, universal values. I am skeptical about that, which is why I ended my review with this: 'As for the covert solidarity of liberal white folks? That is another story. All art, I think, is at some level identity-based, and the more self-aware it is as such, the better.'"
– Interview with Jeffrey Deitch: "And the standards that are here—you can't have a half-baked exhibition and keep your position."
– We have also witnessed the dean of an art academy say during the selection process to admit MFA students: "There are objective standards for good art. Our job is select students who demonstrate these."
– We witnessed an art student say with great frustration when we refused the expression "good art." The student stated: "Everyone knows good art when they see it."

– The Hugo Boss prize:
"Obviously the value of art can't be assessed using a strictly empirical methodology, so the subjective tastes of the jurors inevitably come into play. That said, there are certain criteria that the jury carefully consider. These aren't related to an artist's demographic—their age, nationality, or the mediums they work in—or a specific project, but rather focus on the power and originality of their overall artistic vision. Is the artist somehow shifting the parameters of artmaking? Does his or her work change the way we think about the world? And is it making an enduring impact on younger generations of artists?"

3. W. Haftmann, *Malerei nach 1945. documenta-2-Katalog* (Köln: DuMont Schauberg, 1959), 14.
Poensgen Georg and Leopold Zahn, *Abstrakte Kunst eine Weltsprache* (Baden-Baden: Woldemar Klein, 1958).

4. NASA, "Voyagers to the Stars," *NASA website*. http://spaceplace.nasa. gov/voyager-to-stars.

5. Matthew W. Hughey and Devon R. Goss, "A Level Playing Field? Media Constructions of Athletics, Genetics, and Race," *The Annals of the American Academy of Political and Social Science*, Vol 661, Issue 1, 2015, August 10, 2015. http://ann.sagepub.com/ content/661/1/182.abstract.

6. Komar + Melamid, "The Most Wanted Paintings" *Dia Artist's Web Projects*, 1995. http://awp.diaart.org/km.

7. Hanna Brinkmann, Laura Commare, Helmut Leder, Raphael Rosenberg, "Abstract Art as a Universal Language?" *Leonardo/The MIT Journals* Volume 47, Issue 3 (June 2014): 256-257. doi: 10.1162/LEON_a_00767.

8. Joyce Wadler, "Can Taste Be Taught?," *New York Times*, October 18, 2007. http://www.nytimes. com/2007/10/18/garden/18bunny.html.

9. Jacoba Urist, "Is Good Taste Teachable?," *New York Times*, October 4, 2017. https://www.nytimes. com/2017/10/04/style/design-good-taste.html.

10. Deniz Tekiner, "Art, Power, and Social Change," *Social Justice*, Vol. 33, No. 2, 104 (2006): 40.

11. The Tate, "What is the Turner Prize?," *The Tate Website*. http://www. tate.org.uk/whats-on/tate-britain/ exhibition/turner-prize.

12. Museum of Modern Art New York, "Mission Statement," *MOMA's Website*. http://www.moma.org/about.

13. LACMA and MOCA, "LACMA and MOCA: A Message from Michael Govan," *Unframed*, March 7, 2013. https://unframed.lacma. org/2013/03/07/lacma-and-moca-a-message-from-michael-govan.

AMBIGUISM

In language, and in fields such as science and consciousness, ambiguity seems to be a reality of the human condition. Language unites with poor success rates. The most well-formulated and well-received expression, in a shared language, is an example, and not the exemplary. Ambiguity is important to explore. However, the same aspects of ambiguity that explore meaning and reality, leave it open to hijacking.

Formulating oneself is essential if one wishes to win over an audience, big or small.[1] Even if one is gifted with a straight gaze and a wit, self-formulation is not at all a clear proposition. For every organization of verb and noun there is a lifetime of experiences and narratives that simply cannot be fully translated to another human being with another lifetime of experiences — despite a shared language or even a shared roof. The generic equality that speech creates between humans promises to transmit the distinctiveness of individuals in the abstract, but it is this same distinction between individuals that cannot be transmitted, in the concrete. In addition to the typical stupidity and narcissism, the misinterpretation or reinterpretation of a particular formulation can also be an irreconcilable difference of perspective making it impossible to pull the same meaning from a collection of words as the author/speaker's intentions — simply because of the immense gap in lived experience and therefore in the assumption of meaning and basic definitions of words.

In philosophy a related area is known as heurmaneutics. The hermeneutic circle stresses that meaning in a transmission is found in the context itself. An individual receiving a transmission must try to interpret it using what is known about the context where the transmission was sent. Art history and criticism contends with this while admitting that humanity's temporal narcissism (or at least its myopia) makes it impossible. Distance between individuals and contexts dilutes the transmission.

Meaning and lived truth is lost in the chasm between source and receiver. The most expressible is the most common, and the least unusual, eliminating difference and singularity by default. Things become common through repetition, forming familiarity that may overlap but is not bound to truth or lived experience. When the expression of a familiarized commonality is done on purpose in order to influence, in sociology this is known as framing. Words are not strict containers of reality, but they certainly frame bias. Ideological framing further estranges any transmission, turning it into a tool for manipulation instead of for understanding.

Mundane facts, physical properties, observable phenomenon and theoretical interpretations made through the scientific method also do not guarantee shared communication. Dictionary definitions appear definitive, however even the basics are overrun with belief systems. Only on rare occasions, on few topics, may we overlook discrepancies, opposing perspective and sad cognitive inertia. Moments of birth and death, a meal after a long fast, a sexy glance causing a heart to speed up, a deep sleep after a long day, and the twinkling galaxies of unfathomably deep space — these are some of the precious few truly shared experiences between us, but even these are infinite in variation.

Cosmopolitanism called for a unification of the populations of the world by setting basic universal human rights (hospitality according to Kant, and the right to have rights according to Arendt), however, an assumption of this much responsibility in the abstract collapses with the individual. Cosmopolitan thinking has not managed to contain or eliminate genocide, war crimes, mass murder, localized police brutality, or even common schoolyard bullying. Cosmopolitan thinking developed into globalism, leading multinational corporate entities to evade democratic control, leading to more efficient brutality via expanding webs of framing in order to control masses of people. A universal serial bus is not universal. International market peace (Pax Venalicium) is not peaceful – looking at such pre-failed utopias as the European Union where the Greek and Spanish suicide rates break record highs[2] – and cannot even preclude war (Ukraine, Israel, Syria, Yemen, etc). Everything else is difference, built from singular mono-consciousness and the fact that our life forces are separated from each other. Those universal things floating in the minds of otherwise rational beings are universal only in childish and totalitarian dreams: hypothetical other minds in the abstract. Violence expends itself through the milky way.

WEIRD UNIVERSE

Levi-Strauss suggested that human characteristics are the same everywhere. Joe Henrich's research found otherwise: human psychology and cognition vary around the world, wildly.[3] Psychological differences between people are much, much greater than scientists previously realized. "Universal" psychological traits were drawn from studies that were based on the same people: western, educated, industrialized, rich and democratic, and furthermore, mostly university students, and thus from a limited class range. Humans are different from each other, for example by degree of structural agency and freedom of movement, value systems, social bonds, and the tremendous differences in life experiences that results from these traits. Differences in habitus, geography, and ideology represent permanent barriers between individuals that grow deeper with class and geography.

Perhaps there are exceptions to be made on purely speculative, mathematical, and scientific formulations. However, even the most detached, rational observations, in the form of rows of data, or what Kant attempted by avoiding belles-lettres, are altered by the singularity of consciousness, present knowledge, and ideology as usual. Even repeatable observations are observed from singular, temporal perspectives that may simply be distorted. Science is built on the possibility of repetition and predictability, and is perhaps the closest we will ever come to truly sent and received transmissions. (The Arecibo message was sent into outer space with the hope that science could be a Universal language.) However, science is relatively young, and it revises its findings often enough that its foundations are still called theories, and mathematics grows less certain the further out it goes. While our species has been building an impressive database with factual evidence of the workings of things, no practicing scientist would declare human interpretation of nature to be finished.

The problem with communication may come from the distortion of perspective caused either by a signal getting altered by gravity located between source and receiver, or by the sense/intellect apparatus of the receiver. Heated debates inevitably fog over with ideological misinterpretations of factual evidence. We also don't know what happened before the big bang or what will happen after all the suns burn out and matter spreads out boringly thin across the universe.[4]

All communications are sent from and received by singular perspectives with a unique lifetime of experiences. For every formulation, there is a choice of words, a selection of possibilities. This selection has expressive consequences, no matter how abstract and factual its content. A clear formulation is clear because the sender and receiver share a higher number of commonalities and thus code and decode a transmission with mutual shared recognition.

Even with the most clearly formulated and received transmission, there are large, tragic blind spots. We see this between family members, between colleagues of the same discipline, and naturally, in any public communication, even within a small group of similar people. The gap increases with every change in social class, nationality, religion and every lived experience or lack thereof. This gap between transmission and reception is our unfathomable melancholy: deepest loneliness is the consequence of being a species capable of understanding how alone we are. Our singularity in the crowd is made painfully obvious by anyone who has attempted to address a crowd: all closeness is simulated. The only language that seems to function is the painfully simplistic sentiment built on shared biological and experiential references that are hopelessly vague and unable to transmit any truly individual insight or horror. The only language that can unite a crowd is emotional manipulation: using language as an empty signifier, devoid of content completely, leaving each individual to fill it with what they desire.

EXCEPTIONAL POTENTIAL

Exceptions may be located in isolated groups of people whose world is disconnected from the rest of the world, and whose environment and daily life unfolds slowly, over generations. For example, the people living on North Sentinel Island, violently hostile to any outside attempt to communicate with them, may be able to communicate to one another effectively, who knows. There could be another exception found in the power of one to one communication by slow vehicles such as literature and art where, through time, understanding of a particular formulation matures, and produces a crowd, one mind at a time, decade upon decade, where transmission expands to reach a closer understanding in reception than usual. This occurs based on the weight of discourse around the transmission, and its translation through time, enabling it to acquire its own gravity. Many artists see the potential for open, generous transmissions that do not resort to empty, manipulative, emotional gestures.

Poets, artists, philosophers and others are occasionally able to somehow concretize abstraction and transmit essences that cut through the fog and singularity of the individual surprisingly (comfortingly) moderately large numbers of other people. Through time, people receive, interpret and assimilate these transmissions into something like greater, shared understanding. Even here, comprehension is illusory: the understanding the receiver gains from a particular formulation cannot be exactly the same understanding as the sender of the formulation, but those who are aware of this, leave an emptiness inside the work. The hope is that some essence transfers, a seed of factual evidence and lived experience. The sender must understand that roominess inside a transmission allows multiple singularities to interpret the transmission without losing its essence. This is not the same as universalism: it is its opposite. Acceptance of our singularity — no two crystals form alike — allows us to imagine our position compared to each other. This melancholy acceptance then forms a cloud of individuals who, operating alone together, form something that could be mistaken for a mountain.

PARASITOID DÉMARCHE

It is sadly predictable that the most common motivation for public mutual affect is to achieve leverage and personal gain, and to sell something. The exploitation of our failure to achieve communication especially impacts the political realm where speech inventively simulates reality. In order to do this, our public figures use what we will call parasitoid démarche: the possession of words from our inherited language using the illusion of universality in order to manipulate for ideological motives. A parasitoid exploitation of language is complete the moment when an ideological framing of a concept has completely won, choking the meaning of its host word, killing it from behind: and thus the original meaning of the word has been redefined. General ideological framing then no longer needs to occur, the word has now permanently been changed, its original meaning dead (or at least dormant). Any future framing of this word needs to be done by those who attempt to resuscitate its original, forgotten meaning. We should provide examples here, in an earnest effort to communicate.

The parasitoid démarche works by pretending to shed differences between people by using basic emotional triggers framed as shared experiences and values. In order to formulate expressions that will be interpreted by the largest mass of people in the most favorable way, the burden of factual content is unloaded. Content is made up of facts that cannot be presented in public because the differences in singularity, thus in interpreted perspectives, will radically alter the reception of an intended message in ways that are disadvantageous to the manipulator(s). A master illusionist such as the politician, cannot afford to have explicit fact in a message, and instead relies on feint and icon sold as shared understanding. The parasitoid démarche is based on exploiting the most basic shared biological facts, (hunger for food, avoidance of extreme temperatures) our basic psychological desires (need to love and be loved, fear of the unknown) and our easy to revise shared histories (need to belong to a group) — the few things we share as a species. Ideologues, using a parasitoid démarche attack, take basic vocabulary from our vernacular languages, and with intensive, public reframing, absolutely empty the word of content and then refill it with whatever bunkum needed for the self-advancement of the speaker or those interests the speaker actually represents. The parasitoid démarche uses supposedly basic, shared concepts in order to feign nearness and then obtain the sympathy necessary for the speaker's true motivation: votes, sales, and shadowy self-advancement. Debord discovered this last century: "The flagrant destruction of language is flatly acknowledged as an officially positive value because the point is to advertise reconciliation with the dominant state of affairs–and here all communication is joyously proclaimed absent."[5]

The parasitoid démarche is not jargon. Jargon is another, parallel vocabulary that only specialists understand. The parasitoid démarche uses the same words that everyone "understands". The parasitoid démarche is not propaganda, although they both share emotional triggers. Propaganda does not change the meaning of a word, it uses clever combinations of words in order to influence through emotional triggers. The parasitoid démarche uses known words but it changes the meaning altogether of those words. The spokesman for the National Rifle Association said after yet another school shooting incident in the United States: "the only thing that can stop a bad guy with a gun is a good guy with a gun." That is a propagandistic statement. Each word of that sentence means more or less what it normally would mean in another context. (The words "good" and "bad" are the most troublesome here.) The parasitoid démarche is a much more efficient and insidious way to manipulate, using our shared language, than mere propaganda.

The parasitoid démarche is related to George Orwell's totalitarian language Newspeak, except no new words are invented (such as bellyfeel or upsub), it merely feeds on the body of a familiar word, killing its essence and replacing it with a specific framing.[6]

The difference between Orwell's doublethink is consciousness: parasitoid démarche sinks into the deepest subconscious of the center — at least of those 26% in the United States in 2014 who believed the sun revolves around the earth, and probably more.[7]

Parasitoid démarche requires an individual to actively evade basic, in your face fact such as easy-to-find science and general fact. The cold blooded murder of an unarmed black teen-age kid on his way home from a candy run is warped by the parasitoid demarche "self-defence". The parasitoid démarche no longer requires active thinking at all, since the reframe has been so successful that it has become the accepted meaning of the word. The parasitoid démarche version of "self-defence" expresses the belief that any young black man in the United States is a violent aggressor even if factually this is obviously not true at all.

Words such as security, love, need, danger, entitlement, terrorism, and freedom become something completely different than their dictionary entries. A good, solid, contemporary word felled by the parasitoid démarche is the word "security". We all want and need to be secure, to be protected from those who wish us harm and from the ravages of nature, thus the shared emotional investment in the word. However, after a brutal parasitoid démarche, the word security as currently used is an insidious mixture of oppressive authoritarian invasion of the masses, absolute social control disguised as structural incompetence and epic, theatrical obfuscation of true motives. The word security is invoked whenever oppression is normalized.

Another word that fell to parasitoid démarche, a classic, is "freedom." Since freedom of movement is an essential characteristic of a prosperous life, we all identify with the word one way or another. (The control of oneself, with or without assistance, is essential.) But the word freedom, post parasitoid démarche, means the violent control of an "other". Freedom is also used as an attack against those who dare to fail in a system that is set up to facilitate the failure of a large number of marginalized people within a population as in: "you had the freedom to make the choices you made that caused your own failure in society and in life." (This formulation is also an example of a "double bind".)

We can only describe the techniques used by neoliberalism as an onslaught of double bind psychological attacks using parasitoid démarche vocabulary to refine the warped perspective of reality in which the predators always win and yet claim to be looking out for the best interests of their victims. The art field is also loaded with double bind demands on the artist. "Be unique!" is the verbal rally, while the resource rewards are funneled to the known, iconic, and least other.

The parasitioid démarche is all over the legal system, and perhaps the most vile implementation of it. The legal system has formalized abstraction to a degree as far removed from material fact, ethics, fairness, and humanity as possible. The word innocent no longer means not having murdered someone as in the cases involving the "Stand Your Ground" laws that have been invoked as successful defenses. The word innocent does not mean not having murdered someone as in the countless cases of U.S. police murdering citizens seemingly for sport with the full support of the legal-justice system.

Even the word *person* has fallen victim to the parasitioid démarche. The word person, commonly meaning a *human being*, has been warped to cover inanimate objects as in the "Corporate Personhood" doctrine from the precedent set in 1888: "Under the designation of 'person' there is no doubt that a private corporation is included [in the Fourteenth Amendment]." (Pembina Consolidated Silver Mining Co. v. Pennsylvania, 125 U.S. 394 (1886))

The parasitoid démarche is worldwide. The Confucian concept of harmony, 和 he, imagined an ideal social formation, but when translated into the current parasitoid language inflection means something more like "brutally, totally, absolutely enforced conformity to party lines, no matter how insane, disgusting or cruel, at no expense spared to nation or individual, the air we breathe, or the planet we live on".

Parasitoid démarche moves are not limited to politics and business. It is also not strictly contained to words. Finally, we arrive at the bridge: the insistence in the busy-ness of art that ambiguity is an ideal form is a condition closely related to the parasitoid démarche. We call it ambiguism.

AMBIGUITY

Ambiguity is a natural condition of the universe, that is, clear, mythological meaning and teleological narrative is radically unlikely in nature. Physics advises that we accept the wave-particle duality of matter, ambiguity on atomistic levels. If position x and momentum p cannot be known simultaneously, the uncertainty principle is not an observation of our technological limits, it is in fact, a deeper observation of the ambiguous principles of the universe.

Sincerely searching ambiguity is a courageous choice for an individual who is not afraid of facing and embracing enigma. The Tao Te Ching explores essential yet unnameable properties of the universe, and the deliberately ambiguous text itself invites conflicting interpretations of its contradictory declarations. According to dominant western values, such existential insecurity is interpreted as "feminine" and thus as "weakness" because it is neither goal oriented, nor dogmatically decisive. Thus a westernized artist searching ambiguity is on a tough road, challenging both career and mental health in a world that insists on quantifiable results, use-value, and obtuse brutality. The profound acceptance of ambiguity as a condition of life and the universe is deeply felt by countless artists, writers, and scientists, through history. Samuel Beckett is only one of many whose oeuvre relentlessly explores the conditions of ambiguity.

Since Adorno, Frenkel-Brunswik, Levinson, and Sanford first linked intolerance to ambiguity to the authoritarian personality shortly after World War II,[8] many psychologists and sociologists have concluded that ambiguity intolerance corresponds to a high degree of dogmatic, fearful, culturally intolerant attitudes. "One who is characterized as intolerant of ambiguity tends to view and construe ambiguous situations as a cause of psychological uneasiness or anxiety, or possibly a threat; thus, ambiguity is viewed as confusing and something to avoid."[9]

The art ecosystem's idealization of the ambiguous object stems from the brief moment in time when the embrace of ambiguity was a clearly stated position of enlightened philosophical inquiry against dogma. We will mention only one more example here: COFFEA ARÁBIGA, a 1969 film by Cuban filmaker Nicolás Guillén Landrián.[10] The film managed to disturb Fidel Castro, or at least his censorship team, while functioning nevertheless as propaganda for an ambitious state plan for coffee production. The film appeared to highlight egalitarian relations between races: "in Cuba everyone, black and white, we all drink coffee" while showing that most of the coffee factory workers were marginalized black women. Landrián's position in the Cuban revolutionary state was intellectual and conditional, openly rebelling against demands of orthodox conformity, and yet obviously supportive of its potential. Landrián's use of the censored Beatles' song "Fool on the Hill" in the soundtrack is an impossible object. Was the fool on the hill the filmmaker himself: "the eyes in his head, see the world spinning round"? Or was this song a simple insult to Castro? Did use of the Beatles subvert or promote Cuba's rival system? The ambiguity of the film was intolerable for the censors and stunts like these earned Landrián the electroshock torture he received before escaping to Miami.

AMBIGUISM

In the case of ambiguity in contemporary art, a problem arises because the very nature of an ambiguous production is open to interpretation, it is therefore very easy to hijack, even easier than words.

The origins of ambiguism in idealist, non-western, critical thinking give it the aura of an old, just, revolutionary hero. Tergiversation in the sheep-skin of earnest intellectual pursuit is impossible to criticize head-on since the easy retort "reactionary!" could just as easily be "radical!" as needed. But its very nature leaves ambiguous work open to parasitiod démarche attacks. Art administrators and other gate-keepers have discovered that the "correct" ambiguous work can be political if needed, formal when necessary, spiritual when desirable, and an emotional leverage when convenient. Ambiguism is well-adjusted, fitting comfortably into whatever ideology that claims it. One may fill in the blanks, "discovering" content to reflect one's worldview. Perfect!

THE IMPOSSIBLE OBJECT

"Art for art's sake" is the perfect host for ambiguism. The unspoken, implied role of ambiguism is the exact opposite of freedom, a betrayal of the struggles of its origins. There are two stages. First stage ambiguism is when sincerely ambiguous objects are hijacked. Second stage ambiguism is where the art field simply produces well-adjusted, empty formalism, with an implied but never landing "critique", ready to be filled with anything, hijack-ready. This second, cynical stage of ambiguism feigns ambiguity while propping up the realist-conformist view. Second-stage ambiguism is made to be used, ready to be used, hopes to be used, pines wistfully to be used. The art object itself may be more or less ambiguous, and more or less nice to look at, well-done, and crafty, but the structure that makes it possible and visible is absolutely lucid, as solid, concrete and functional as the Three Gorges Dam. The structure frames all objects, but especially those displaying ambiguism: correct, non-threatening, familiarized yet still stimulating because of the emaciated symbols of rebellion they weakly radiate. Ambiguism reduces transmissions to the most shared, least differentiated or individuated gestures which then become effortlessly occupied. Unlike a sincere, philosophical embrace of ambiguity, contemporary art displaying ambiguism wants to sell itself to almost everyone, the largest group, (or sub-group) like a politician and Madison Avenue. Ambiguism asserts that one cannot afford to lose the mainstream with potentially uncomfortable, mal-adjusted, party-pooping content. It relies on visceral reaction to form, via very slight biological, psychological and historical cues to produce an empathic response spiced up by the sexy and inflated "mystery" of artistic creation corresponding to the biographical chilli-pepper footnotes of Genii and the myth of genius. The desired response is so basic, so crude, that it is easy to disguise within sexy, mysterious gestures.

Art displaying ambiguism is not always produced, by the artist, primarily for this purpose. Furthermore, ambiguism is often agreeable, enjoyable and legitimately entertaining, rich, full, smart, and fun. This is the result of appealing to the widest base — and it is therefore difficult to simply dismiss all together. Ambiguism is, after all, the contemporary art of our time.

1. This text was formulated and revised well before Trump began his successful run for CEO of the United States of America. After reading and thinking through this text again, we decided to change or add nothing, because Trump's methods were classical, completely unoriginal in the history of power and manipulation.

2. Pam Harrison, "Greek Debt Crisis: Tragic Spike in Suicide Rates," *Medscape*. December 6, 2015. http://www.medscape.com/viewarticle/846904.
Also: Diego Fonseca, "Number of suicides doubles that of road deaths in Spain for first time," El País, April 1, 2016.
http://elpais.com/elpais/2016/03/31/inenglish/1459424492_066337.html.

3. Joe Henrich, Steven J. Heine, and Ara Norenzayan, "The Weirdest People in the World?," *Working Paper Series des Rates für Sozial- und Wirtschaftsdaten*, No. 139 (May 7, 2010).
http://dx.doi.org/10.2139/ssrn.1601785.

4. We have a hypothesis: like 1979 video game Asteroids where matter going off screen left arrives back onscreen right, but infinitely large: matter in the universe floats off before it gathers again in the center and explodes back off screen again — a loop, not a line. Our universe is an infinite animated .gif.

5. Guy Debord, *Society of the Spectacle* (Detroit, Black and Red Press, 1977), 192.

6. George Orwell, *Nineteen Eighty-Four* (London: Martin Secker & Warburg, 1949), 32.

7. National Science Foundation, "Chapter 7. Science and Technology: Public Attitudes and Understanding," National Science and Engineering Indicators, 2014.
http://www.nsf.gov/statistics/seind14/content/chapter-7/c07.pdf.

8. Theodor W. Adorno, Else Frenkel-Brunswik, Daniel Levinson, Nevitt Sanford, *The Authoritarian Personality* (New York: Harper & Brothers 1950).

9. Katya Stoycheva "Tolerance for Ambiguity, Creativity, and Personality" *Bulgarian Journal of Psychology* (2010): 6.
http://rcp2009.files.wordpress.com/2009/10/bjop20101-4-seercp2009-papers_part_two-910-pages.pdf.

10. Search the internet for a bad print of this film that nevertheless conveys its power.

27
CATEGORIES

Clear and Light

Hoary and Rich

Divine and Sexy

Steady and Wise

Usual and Novel

Huge and Dumb

Lofty and Chatty

Light and Distant

Moist and Clingy

Barren and Frigid

Early and Unhewn

Slimy and Detailed

Devious and Needy

Plain and Awkward

Bright and Carefree

Simple and Concise

Loving and Unlucky

Personal and Skillful

Penetrating and Calm

Mysterious and Foggy

Beautiful and Gracious

Etherial and Numinous

Melancholic and Wealthy

Vigorous and Upstanding

Relentless and Optimistic

Handsome and Refreshing

Refined and Conscientious

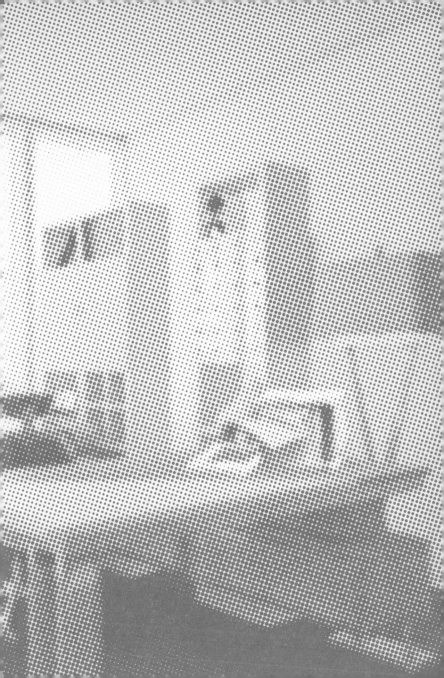

AESTHETICS
OF
PSYCHOPATHY

The Aesthetics of Psychopathy is the ideal mode of practicing Genii. We use the plural of genius to highlight its inflation and effusive dispersion. Even if we suspend our disbelief in the mystical construction of genius — especially inflated in art — it is not possible for any particular generation or milieu to produce as many Genii as is necessary to keep the busy-ness of art running efficiently. Therefore, standards for demonstrating the signs of genius are defined and enforced. The signs of the Genii are the aesthetics of Genii. The aesthetics of Genii are in flux, not quite seasonally, but almost. The signs of Genii are interchangeable with the signs of privilege, which are interchangeable with the signs of victory.

The concept is cheap, but somehow genius holds eternal, mythical reverence. E.H. Gombrich wrote in his The Story of Art: "One cannot explain the existence of genius. It is better to enjoy it."[1]

Genius is a self-fulfilling prophecy, religious in its fundament, speaking more about those who declare it. Dissected by mainstream science, genius, and its necessary opposite, failure, (including failed genetics) is sprinkled around in policy and "common sense" politics in widespread, yet difficult to pin down areas of life and governance that include the relatively minor, but wholly representative field known as the art ecosystem. One could perhaps plead a case for genius in science where individuals are able to do complex mathematics in their heads.[2] However in many fields, such as art, the contingencies are epic and the mechanisms to assign the honour are dodgy social constructions that are widely and faithfully believed as observed facts of nature. The root of the word genius comes from the ancient Roman "guiding spirit" of a person or place. Related to the verb genui, to create, the achievements of exceptional individuals indicated the presence of a particularly powerful tutelary deity, and thus the word gradually through time began to mean innate "inspiration" and "talent" generally. It is notable that the origin of the word began in incense-reeking mysticism.

HEGEL'S STUPIDITY

In the spirit of Hegel, let's go back to examine two important sources for the concept of genius that we are stuck with today: Hegel and Galton. Hegel wrote endlessly stupid comments about genius, all hopelessly soaked in the limited knowledge of his time, yet his voice echoes in the present. "Therefore this artistic creation, like art throughout, includes in itself the aspect of immediacy and naturalness, and this aspect it is which the subject cannot generate in himself but must find in himself as immediately given. This alone is the sense in which we may say that genius and talent must be inborn."[3] A sentence such as this was clearly written centuries before researchers compiled and analysed data on cognitive development and genetic determinism. Hegel's statements are racist rubbish unsupported by science, clearly buttressing white, northern European supremacy:[4]

"The Italians... have song and melody almost by nature..."
"Modern Greeks... are even now a people of poetry and songs..."
"Thus improvisers are especially at home in Italy and their talent is marvellous."[5]

He concludes these enlightened passages with brilliance: "In this way art and its specific mode of production hangs together with the specific nationality of peoples."[6]

What Hegel also failed to grasp is that values are formed by specifics of a public in an ecosystem that has nothing to do with race biology (that is anyway constructed.)[7] He drones on about the "natural inspiration" of a genius, without understanding the environment in which genius is evaluated as such. Statements such as these mine the depths of stupidity: scientific racism unfortunately contributed to the formation of views of genius and talent up to the present.

GALTON'S STUPIDITY

The word gradually expanded its explicitly race-based connotations through the enlightenment until it became a questionable tool of Francis Galton who used dodgy statistics to outline the distribution of intelligence in a population.

Galton's "research" led him to the "scientific" identification of people on the high end of the bell-curve who were gifted with the genes of "natural ability of intellect and disposition" — genius. Galton's anthropometric measures are at the root of today's IQ tests and college entrance exams. According to the Binet Scale of Human Intelligence a genius is someone with an IQ Score of over 140.

However, on the lower end of the scale, Galton developed a physiognomic system of criminality by superimposing photos to find average features of criminal types. Although physiognomy was practiced since at least ancient Greece, Galton's systematic, easy to apply framework contributed to the field of eugenics. Supporters of the practice wanted to implement improvements of the "genetic composition of a population." These geniuses included Winston Churchill, H. G. Wells, Theodore Roosevelt, John Maynard Keynes and Adolph Hitler, among many, many others arranged across all levels of power and policy. After no small amount of death, misery, oppression and massive, avoidable despair, (after all, racism and class domination is not a tsunami or an earthquake or other such natural disaster), by the mid 20th century eugenics finally became pejoratively known as "scientific racism." Unfortunately, this was quite some time after many institutions, educational structures, and class systems were firmly cemented into place, remaining mostly so until today.[8]

Galton wrote that it would be "quite practicable to produce a highly-gifted race of men by judicious marriages during several consecutive generations." Scandinavian leaders perked up at this idea, implementing disgusting legislation at the recommendation of, to name only one example, the Svenska sällskapet för rashygien (the Swedish Society for Racial Hygiene).[9] Although they toned the name down a little to the Swedish Institute for Race Biology, it instituted the radical forced sterilization program from 1922 until 1975 for those "not worthy to have children." Passed by vote in the democratic Swedish Parliament, these policies targeted "deficient", "deviant", "imbecilic", and other "undesirable" people who included mixed-race individuals, gypsies, single mothers, and any other potentially non-conformist traits in the population that could just include a wide spectrum of people: from people with a physical or intellectual difference to political dissidents. Most of these programs were formally abolished in 1976. (Demokrati!) However still today, Sweden has mandatory forced sterilization before sex change surgery as a condition to give a trans gender person official ID papers.

SCHOPENHAUER'S STUPIDITY

Who are Genii, and how are they recognized? Since even Schopenhauer was convinced that genius was stamped in the physiognomy of "him (sic) who is gifted with it", it follows logically that the simulation and inflation of genius into Genii would place the greatest importance on physical characteristics that can be read by an eager public who is not reacting consciously to the procedure. Schopenhauer suggested that freedom from self-subjection is a sure-fire way to distinguish the face of a genius from the face of someone with reasonable prudence. A genius is someone in a "natural" privilege to dominate. A certain tasty, cool, lack of scruples should therefore be inscribed in the face of Genii who are ready to do anything to get what they want. Ethics and other "do the right thing" narratives are considered degenerate, naive, passé, quaint, strictly for losers, and should only be paid cruelly curled lip service. Genius and privilege run together in mutual support. "Nothing personal, it's just business", "playing hardball", "making the tough choices," "crunching the numbers", "very competitive", "survival of the fittest", "innovative," "disruption," "development," "you're fired!" etcetera — there are far too many expressions for the black hole where empathy is hurled.

THE AESTHETICS OF PSYCHOPATHY

Genii aesthetics demand the annihilation of equity and empathy. This condition is necessary if the vile maxim is the only way to survive in such a "competitive" environment as the busy-ness of art, other industries such as FIRE, and really any field in the battlefields of neoliberal capitalism. Most Genii are not actually psychopathic, that is, they do not have clinical imbalances in their brains, but instead must learn to emulate psychopathy in order to compete. Genii aesthetics is therefore an emulation of the inherent psychopathy of the Vile Maxim. ("All for ourselves, and nothing for other people, seems, in every age of the world, to have been the vile maxim of the masters of mankind.")[10]

The Vile Maxim is further demonstrated by how few stars there are in the constellation making up Genii Valhalla. In the rare case where true neural psychopathy exists in Genii (as in, decreased amygdala response), these individuals prowl as ideal leaders in their natural habitat among the majority who merely feign.

Our cloudy hunch concretized as pop-sci in the middle of writing this text: a study published in Scientific American declared that "if you have psychopathic traits (yes, as in those shared by serial killers) such as being aggressive and emotionally tough, you are more likely to be considered a genius."[11] Notice the author wrote "more likely to be considered a genius." She did not write: "more likely to be able to do complex maths in your head." The performance of genius is a pose to be recognized by people who would not understand the more complex contributions of people more gifted than themselves.

Although there are women psychopaths, it is worth noting that the Aesthetics of Psychopathy crosses into what is increasingly referred to as toxic masculinity, which is of course, the performance of rigid gender expectations. The myth of genius assumes a performance of the masculine asshole. In reality, male behaviour ranges the full spectrum of empathy and action. However, in toxic masculinity, the emulation of psychopathy is the mythic ideal of the alpha-monster, male archetype.

CLINICAL PSYCHOPATHY

Here are a few facts as currently known in order to establish a working definition of the word psychopath. Clinical diagnoses are made by looking at several competing checklists. All of these definitions are heavily debated, but let's have a look at the three most used psychopathy models to compare commonalities.

The Psychopathic Personality Inventory (PPI) list:

Social influence. Fearlessness. Stress immunity. Machiavellian egocentricity. Rebellious nonconformity. Blame externalization. Carefree nonplanfulness. Coldheartedness.

The PCL-R list:

Glibness/superficial charm. Grandiose sense of self-worth. Pathological lying. Cunning/manipulative. Lack of remorse or guilt. Shallow affect (genuine emotion is short and egocentric). Callousness; lack of empathy. Failure to accept responsibility for own actions.

The Triarchic model:

Boldness, low fear including stress-tolerance, disinhibition, poor impulse control, meanness, lacking empathy and close attachment.

There are physical, observable differences between the brains of psychopaths and not psychopaths. MRI and PET scans of a brain with psychopathy indicate decreased amygdala responses that result directly in decreased fear and empathy.[12] However, in most Genii, the same decreased amygdala response is unlikely. Psychopathic behavior is a learned posture necessary to compete in a system such as neoliberal capitalism. So, in the same way that some young Thais, South Koreans, Indians, and Mexicans use whitening cream in order to emulate the more culturally "valuable" white skin they see on fashion models — artists (and curators, and bankers, and increasingly anyone ambitious from any profession) simulate decreased amygdala responses in order to fulfil the classical, ruthless stereotype of genius.

With no small amount of perverse irony, being a true psychopath does prepare one for social battlefield earth where neoliberalism turned living into an extreme sport. The emulation of psychopathy is thus a potential winning formula for what is considered to be success. Sociologists J.J. Ray and J.A.B. Ray stated that "Psychopaths seem to have in abundance the very traits most desired by normal persons. When so many so-called normal individuals attend assertiveness training, the untroubled self-confidence of the psychopath seems almost like an impossible dream. When many young persons are feeling the need for social skills training, the magnetic attraction of the psychopath for members of the opposite sex must seem almost supernatural."[13] Focused action in stressful environments leads to higher success ratios that put psychopaths (and high performing emulators) in higher and higher positions. "A psychopathic strategy doesn't just code for greater success in the bedroom. It also comes in handy in the boardroom."[14]

ICY SUCCESS OR TEPID ALTRUISM

The Aesthetics of Psychopathy became Genii Aesthetics when neoliberal capitalism became the fully implemented ideology. First, since there is only enough "room" in the structure for a few at the top, (mirroring society as a whole) candidates for Genii must be easily identifiable by demonstrating behavior such as narcissism and vile-maxim hoarding. The action of resource distribution via gate-keeping must be streamlined, like every other industrial and complex networked system. In this way, artists must be earmarked for future success and status as Genii. Furthermore, and most importantly, the vile-maxim, absence of empathy, distaste for ethics and winner-take-all ruthlessness are the defining features of the ruling-classes, made ever more concentrated in neoliberalism. Since the resources of the art field are the playthings of the upper classes, they demand Genii Aesthetics because they are relatable, desirable, and furthermore dutifully reflect the ruling classes. The middle classes then become the middle managers of the Aesthetics of Psychopathy, making "well adjusted" decisions based on appearances and the constantly updated new normal.

The caricature of a success story in business, politics, management, and culture is achieved by absolute cruelty, and the absence of shame or fear. Ruthlessness is seen as performing at a higher level of control and responding to a higher calling — the tutelary deity of ancient times. The Genii performing "in the zone", that is, with a lowered heart rate, increased focus, and fearlessness, should be emulated as closely as possible. Those who most succeed in emulating coolness under pressure are deemed coolest, especially in the busy-ness art ecosystem where otherwise, it seems, most artists are distastefully and pathetically empathic.

That is the incongruity here: artists, according to Timothy Dutton's "Great British Psychopath Survey"[5] are number 7 of the 10 least psychopathic professions. Although this Internet survey is not very rigorous, it is close to self-evident that artists, poets, social workers, nurses and teachers would have much fewer psychopaths in their ranks than other more sexy, lucrative and combative professions such as business, law and finance. The poor, artist-poet type is uncomfortably empathic, overly sensitive and unpalatable for public taste that prefers ice-cold anti-heroes with money. Psychopathic aesthetics, rock star, and CEO behaviours are desirable traits in an artist Genii because they are relatively scarce resources, and because they are normalized as winning.

Researchers Kraus, Côté, and Keltner, in a study on empathic accuracy, concluded that lower-class individuals are simply more empathic than upper-class individuals. Their paper in the journal *Psychological Science* states: "Lacking resources and control, lower-class individuals tend to focus on the external, social context to understand events in their lives. As a result, they orient to oth-er people to navigate their social environments."[6] Empathy and shame are located disproportionately in the lower-classes, a stain that should not touch art: genius must operate at higher levels.

In art, value is set in the competitive structures that pit artists against one another. The Aesthetics of Psychopathy are part of the intensely thickening blasé smog covering human relations.

ART AND THE AESTHETICS
OF PSYCHOPATHY

We should give concrete examples here. The problem with this act is that we need to frame it so it appeals to as many people as possible so our formula may be applied across taste lines. While our portrait of Genii may be accurate in general concept, our examples will be personally biased and therefore tint the entire outline. We therefore unhesitatingly offer Damien Hirst as our example of an artist Genii. There are very few critical thinkers left in the world who back the work, so we are safe here. We could have offered Santiago Sierra, although maybe that exam-ple is just too easy. We would have offered Norwegian Bjarne Melgaard, but he remains somewhat of an art underdog, and seems to have some fans, so we'll let it go. We would have offered Melgaard because of his naked lust to be alpha dog, dominant and unregulated in a 1980's cocain-yacht-party on steroids car-icature of the vile maxim in action, especially after reading this tragically stupid line a curator mumbled about him to the New York Times: "He has a voracious appetite, and he likes his free-dom."[7] We could have mentioned that his performed self-pre-sentation of merciless, hyper-masculine egomania is the spitting image for the neoliberalism on Wall-Street. We could note that his NAMBLA, child soldier works, and the racist chair sculpture declare that he is entitled to traffic in any image, including and especially other people's suffering, without the distasteful, overly empathic burden of criticality or content beyond shock. But no, we'll drop that subject in order to win sympathy for our concept, and because of the divine right to "freedom of expression." Because Melgaard dismisses criticism of his work as homophobia, he thus cannot be criticized because, according to that logic, a queer man cannot also be a neoliberal asshole trafficking in the Aesthetics of Psychopathy. We'll stick with Damien Hirst as our case example because his work traffics in death – the standard psychopathy test bombards a subject with horrifying images of dead and dying while monitoring whether emotion-based brain activity is present.

The other example that we will name comes from poetry. Vanessa Place is a criminal appeals lawyer who specializes in defending people convicted of rape. As poetry, she appropriates explicit details from the cases and frames them as appropriated ready-mades. Her aesthetic as described in her own words: "I did trials very early on and found them intellectually unsatisfying because a trial was mostly performance. It was fun but it didn't have that same working through the maze, the sur-and under-ground labrynth, and what I liked about appeals was there's a way in which you're working within a fiction and you're writing a fiction at the same time and thus building a fiction."[18] Civil codes function because of their generality, their extreme detachment from individual human life. Abstraction is the fundament of our legal system. In the name of fairness and justice, acts are reconstructed in a fictional battleground where all contestants have two desires: to win, and to faithfully reproduce the structure. Truth and justice are hopelessly idealistic, impossible together, and thus a formal proxy is performed in the name of civilization. As a lawyer, Place plays to win. And as a poet, Place plays with the moral certainty of absolute, bloodless detachment, refusing a drop of empathy, ridiculing emotion, affect and sentiment as the weaknesses of lesser beings and maudlin poets.

Popular fascination for legal dramas is driven by delight in labyrinthine fictions populated by psychopaths with alien nerves of steel. There are at least two common TV psychopaths: one is careless enough to get caught doing something illegal, and the second psychopath is the lawyer who is clever enough to bend the rules to defeat the system, for or against a criminal psychopath. The "good" psychopath or the "bad" psychopath: it fluctuates by episode, and is framed either as a dodged bullet or a cruel systemic failure. By dancing with verbal and legal abstractions that are pure intellectual gamesmanship, the main players rarely allow themselves even feigned empathy towards anyone (there is usually a foil character who emotes pathetically for the sake of the audience). Vanessa Place, not coincidentally, has written an episode for the hit television show "Law and Order." The plot summary is as follows: "A 9 year old child's asphyxiated body is found in a suitcase on a bus, with evidence of having been in the Everglades. The coroner found she had a quality nose job."[9] We refuse to speculate whether Place is a psychopath herself, but by looking at her production and self-positioning, it is clear that she traffics primarily in the Aesthetics of Psychopathy that is shamelessly, hopelessly mainstream in the United States of America here in the early 21st century. Any pretention of criticality here is a necessary artifice to maintain a polite froth of civility before committing to further normalizing horror.

In naming these examples, our main intention is not to critique, shame or call out individually an artist who cultivates the Aesthetics of Psychopathy. In our current circumstances, artists who demonstrate Genii Aesthetics are playing the game to win —criticize the game, not the player — and we refuse to demonize or place über responsibility on their shoulders. The more serious and disturbing issue here is the ecosystem: what kind of monstrous ideology produces an ecosystem that normalizes, rewards and emulates psychopathy? A detached abstraction towards life is increasingly normalized across advanced cultures. The indifference of the average North American and European towards drone strikes in foreign countries is abhorrent. The indifference of the average EU citizen towards the mass murders in Syria is abhorrent. The indifference of the average world citizen towards the horrors happening in Yemen is abhorrent. Although we have been formulating this text since 2011, new levels of crisis have been reached after the clear victory of the Aesthetics of Psychopathy in the 2016 US election.[20] The emotions of the masses are too easy to manipulate, by sometimes turning them up high, and sometimes deadening them to oblivion.

Adaptation of the signs of genii is a severe blockage of imagination via internalized censorship. This occurs when an individual recognizes what must be done to gain the resources necessary to survive rather than struggle with the long-term negative consequences of consciousness. This act is cynical and also self-harming since what is gained does not equal what is lost.

THE FAMILIARITY BIAS

The content or actual contribution a Genii makes may be more or less valuable, but secondary. Let us repeat that: an artist who has been declared a Genii may or may not contribute something to humanity, but this does not matter in the present. The most valuable contribution of the Genii is to embody evidence of supremacy of the dominant class. The products of Genii may or may not be easy sell, but they must be promoted. The Genii are promoted by repetition: familiarity created by mere exposure becomes evidence of genius. How else can the mountains of ho-hum products be explained? The art ecosystem seems to run primarily on the familiarity bias fallacy, which is certainly not limited to advertising and pop music.

At an art school in Oslo we saw the beginning of a lecture where a slide with the name of a ubiquitous white male heterosexual local artist with psychopathic tendencies was projected in large letters on the wall. We left bored soon after, but when we walked past the classroom four hours later, the "lecture" had not moved on, the same slide still projected! This particular artist had had 2 solo exhibitions locally that year, and every time he sneezed at home or abroad, the local art professionals declared each spray the freshest. If the students would learn anything that day it would be reverence for this artist's name. This structure of constant reinforcement happens on all levels and all regions of the art ecosystem with shifting specific elements. Mere exposure leads to more exposure — familiarity is mistaken for quality and genius declared as though it were a property of physics. Reality is even more extreme than Debord's statement: "that which appears is good, that which is good appears. The attitude which it demands in principle is passive acceptance which in fact it already obtained by its manner of appearing without reply, by its monopoly of appearance."[21] Contemporary art is a cottage industry and legitimation mechanism of the Society of the Spectacle. The mere exposure effect in many cases is limited to those who are so entitled to "recognize." Hannah Arendt, tracing aristocratic race-thinking to racism, wrote about European Romanticism's "unlimited idolization of the 'personality' of the individual, whose very arbitrariness became the very proof of genius."[22]

A 2016 MIT call for applications for a professorship in art listed among their most important minimum qualifications that the candidate must be an "internationally-known artist."[23] MIT would not stoop to use the vulgar word "famous" because it wishes to rise above the bloody vacuity of the Kardashians.

The mere exposure bias also explains eventual backlash against over-exposed artists, (see D. Hirst) necessitating new "classics" which regularly arrive as if by magic, and just on time. One recorded effect of this bias is that after too many repeated exposures, people grow weary and want to move on.[24]

The familiarity bias hurts even the artists who have made it to the Hall of Fame: aging "internationally-known" artists are expected to perform their greatest hits on demand. The market will not allow them to push, and they risk consequences if they do.

HERDING

It is not only mere exposure that generates buzz: tech savvy Gate-Keepers exploit people's tendency to follow the herd. Sociologists Matt Salganik and Duncan Watts observed people downloading and favorably rating music with the highest downloads and ratings, even if it had been rigged with random ratings and downloads from the beginning. They wrote: "We investigated this paradox experimentally, by creating an artificial "music market" in which 14,341 participants downloaded previously unknown songs either with or without knowledge of previous participants' choices. Increasing the strength of social influence increased both inequality and unpredictability of success. Success was also only partly determined by quality: the best songs rarely did poorly, and the worst rarely did well, but any other result was possible."[25] In other words, the songs with the barest threshold had the same chances of exponential success as those obviously accomplished in other "measurable qualities." Herding such as this is accomplished in the art world by the middle managers circulating the same products throughout the global outposts with the matter of fact statement that their pet Genii are already in circulation in the other global outposts and thus their selection was a matter of consensus.

GENII AND MORE GENII

And like this, alternative forms of ingenuity and nourishment are systematically repressed. The most efficient method to do this is to deny resources — everything from attention, space, job positions, and cash — thus stunting the potential lives of individuals, groups and whole populations, and hindering developments in the field along alternative, speculative lines for the benefit of everyone. Time is a luxury that must be spent developing, displaying and performing the body and mind discipline of Genii aesthetics. An independent thinker working with other values is easily marginalised until time and distance render their ideas harmless, then useful, and they can be absorbed to provide novelty, or an ethically perfumed cover-up of the shit-show and ever-mutating spectacle of Genii aesthetics.

Between the public's sad tendency to be attracted to psychopaths in general,[26] various cognitive biases, and the politics of probability, we begin to understand the busy-ness of art is very much like the psychology of irrational exuberances and panic exits of the market. Of course it is! Although this process is a social construction with bellic engines, it cleverly cloaks itself in the language of natural selection in order to appear to be a simple rule of physics or applied computer science.

ARTFACTS.NET

Artfacts.net imagines a unified art world where all the players are on the same field and have the same goal: to top this list (or other similar online rankings that we do not have the time or inclination to write about here). This imaginary unification denies the fact that artists today do not even practice the same profession as the top ranked artists, and often not with those ranked on similar levels. There is no commonality to be compared between Picasso and any working artist today except the presence or lack of fame, which, in itself does not indicate a shared field or a shared goal. Fame via mere-exposure is the primary characteristic of the top artists — life is not even a shared commonality, since many artists on this list are long dead, and many such as Bruce Nauman seem more like ghosts, contributing chill winds. Artfacts. net measures the familiarity bias. While it is seductive to quantify, the flat structure promoted by algorithmic gatekeeping is an illusion based on a convenient, simplifying myth supported by, in this instance, computer science. Artfacts.net tallies mere-exposure from closed, expired circles — it cannot even accurately calculate the new click-bait attention economy and it certainly cannot recognize extra-institutional forms of life.

Artfacts.net cannot and will not include off-site venues in its tallies, even if those sites are the internet itself. Although artfacts. net was programmed in the early 2000's, the algorithm is set up to follow earlier Genii aesthetics before forms such as performance art were absorbed by the mainstream. Singular events of performance art are not calculated in the ranking at all. Marina Abramovic at the MOMA is calculated because the performance was several months in duration at a hyper-exposed, authoritative venue. However, anything taking place in an off-the-map location, no matter how many people see it, or how influential it is, does not register: artfacts.net describes it thusly:

"Public interventions are unfortunately not included in the ranking calculation process because the ranking needs a) an authoritative body like a gallery or museum with a physical address and b) the time period of an exhibition has to be at least 5 days."

We now know that for anything to be art, it must be under authority and last at least 5 days. The Warhol-Picasso-Nauman-Richter-Munch constellation set the primary value source in July 2012. We would then point out that despite the impressive mathematical formulas of artfacts.net, the top artists ranked on artfacts.net are myths. Ranking mortal people alongside mythological people is very creative, or at least superhuman in the same way that applying Jesus Christ or Santa Claus to any current situation is creatively supernatural. Artfacts.net changed their algorithm in 2012 because they said the top hadn't changed in a while. By January 2013 the new top 5 was as follows: Warhol-Picasso-Nauman-Beuys-Richter. (Bye, Munch!) Here is the explanation taken from their website:

"We saw that the Top 100 ranking had become rather static. Static in the sense that all the points artists accumulated for exhibitions never got deleted by the system. Thus, the Artist Ranking algorithm advocated expansionary points accumulation over time. Through this kind of inflationism some artists gained huge amounts of points over the years leading to a kind of monopoly. Rankings did not change at all between 2011 and 2012. From our point of view this loss of dynamics no longer served to accurately reflect the vivid contemporary art world of today. The depreciation is computed using the straight-line method to keep the mathematics simple."

Yes, the mathematic principle is very simple, however the mythological assumptions at work here are epic and faith-based. In the same web page, Artfacts posed the following rhetorical question: "How can you compare a living contemporary video artist with a deceased photographer who was mainly active in the 50s and 60s?" No answer is given, none expected.

In an interview, Marek Claassen, co-founder and director of artfacts.net explains the algorithm:

"80% of the private collectors want oil paintings but many of these artists vanish because they are not accepted in the curatorial environment. There's a big hype for Chinese paintings, people spend millions on it, but it is just design. Artfacts.net reflects the curator's point of view."[27]

Let's ignore that Claassen here made a nationalist and taste-based preference in his supposedly objective calculations. How else does he justify the calculations posted on his website?

"Quality, is the most used term in the art world, rendering its application effectively meaningless."

True, quality is overrated, but fame on the other hand is not. Claassen, in the same interview, takes an easy shot at Damien Hirst (as we already mentioned Hirst is safe to criticise) saying that he doesn't make the top 5 on artfacts.net because sales aren't the sole indicator of quality (see how that works?).[28] "Attention in the cultural world is an economy unto itself, but one that functions with the same mechanisms as capitalism." It is a brilliant and worn strategy, to turn against the market in the name of the market: punk rock! Does a double negative produce a positivist? No it does not. Hirst rests comfortably in the top 100, and this algorithm is programmed with great specificity.

Duchamp, Picasso and Warhol are, by any other ranking, especially academic citation, the Hindu triad of deities in the art ecosystem. Warhol and Picasso are ranked top two, on artfacts. net, but where is Duchamp? The Google Scholar Citations Gadget, the algorithm that counts citations in scholarly publications, lists 16,380 citations for Duchamp, 4,618 for Warhol, 4,606 for Picasso, and 110 for Damien Hirst. However, artfacts.net puts Duchamp at number 35, three spots worse than Hirst who sits at number 32 (as of January 2013). Why is Duchamp at that rank? Duchamp sits below Hirst because he made fewer objects in his career, and there are less "original" objects in circulation. Everyone, by now, has seen urinal, the wine rack, and the bicycle wheel mounted on the chair, at least in reproduction: there is no formulaic variation to fill the world with new-to-you Duchamp objects. Warhol and Picasso, on the other hand, were art factories, pumping out brand recognizable product in large (but still artesian) supply. You can see a new-to-you Picasso painting on every museum outing for decades: their mere-exposure is biblical, their auction prices are phenomenon, and their works have become reliquary evidence of their days as mortals walking the earth. Thus the artfacts.net algorithm is brute fame + units shifted (weighted by price) = brand recognition ranking.

In his claim to avoid the word "quality", and thus the concept of "taste" Claassen quantifies and unifies the tastes of the gatekeepers without naming names or identifying ideologies. Taste is democratized like Athens had a democracy: only the "citizen" has a vote. The ideology that he does not name is neoliberalism, the systematic implementation of the vile-maxim, in this case, across museums, galleries and art centers around the world. In a blog post on Rafael Rosendaal's website he wrote: "Success seems exponential to me... exponential growth... it's hard to imagine how one artist makes hardly any money and another artist can build a multi billion dollar franchise."[29]

IN THE RARE EVENT OF
A CLASSICAL EXAMPLE

When someone appears on the scene who would qualify as a genius according to classical myth, that person is appreciated with acolytes instead of actually being entrusted with policy or position. To use an example outside the art field, (and thus navigate attacks that will focus on specific art and artists we appear to be panning or advocating which is not the goal of this text) we are thinking of Tim Berners-Lee, the guy who invented HTTP, the open infrastructure of the World Wide Web. Most people and governments marginalize the insight that made the internet explode in the first place, allowing more and more of the internet into proprietary, hereditary and corralled private ownership.

Among Shopenhauer's rubbish comments, this one offers insight into human behaviour that could be applied here. "In no case can people receive from his mind more than a reflection, and then only when he joins with them in the attempt to get his thought into their heads; where, however, it is never anything but an exotic plant, stunted and frail."[30] The problem with (something approaching) genius is very basic: it operates far above those sitting on power who are mostly incapable of recognizing it. Is the Federal Communications Commission cynically quid pro quo with the giant internet service providers such as Comcast, or are they simply too stupid to understand how the Berners-Lee open internet has aided humanity? Genius is created on mythological premises, but when someone partially satisfies even those, they are shelved in honour as destabilizing security threats, their feats unfathomable, their names entering long lists of harmlessly boring facts. "Thanks for that genius you dropped, now accept this golden muzzle." Compare the status and financial earnings of Mr. Berners-Lee with Mr. Zuckerberg: only one of them is chummy with Wall Street. Only one of them has a lobbying machine with the ear of the Prime Ministers of England and Presidents of the United States and the Dutch Parliament. Only one of them was trotted out like a harmless puppet during the ceremony of the London Olympics. "This is for everyone" tweeted TimBL into LED lights in the London audience: and yet "this" is increasingly owned by, as Bruce Sterling calls Apple/Google/Facebook, "the Stacks," increasingly untouchable by the masses, the internet was invented to unite. HTTP was created altruistically for the greater advancement of the entire world. Facebook was created to exploit the psychological pathologies of the masses for immense personal gain and deeply penetrating social surveillance. TimBL gets honorary awards and Zuckerberg gets epic cash and real power. One of them is a household name, the other is a nerd-only name on the lists of People Who Could Have Been Billionaires. One of them traffics in psychopathic aesthetics, and the other one seems like a nice guy. Of course, this has to do with the mechanics of kleptocratic neoliberalism, but the point here is that Genii and the Aesthetics of Psychopathy are generated by the same source. Tim Berners-Lee did the improbable action of refusing to oppress: he saw that his invention was a powerful tool for the advancement of everyone across all social stratification lines. His choice was a direct strike to the rule of society that depends on mass ignorance, diffused voice, and lack of agency. Zuckerberg on the other hand, was an opportunist: he saw how his technology could put him at the top of the hierarchy of control, and he seized his moment to be an oppressor, and has stayed there grinning at the top. The markets rewarded him with dramatic riches because the Masters-of-the-Universe saw Facebook as the most powerful tool for surveillance, persuasion and advanced psychopathy in history.

MATHS IN THE HEAD

We prefer not to name a classical genius figure from the current art ecosystem because our criteria will be attacked instead of our methodology. We also do not wish to inadvertently muddle up our own taste with this formulation. So, we prefer to name another computer genius, they are after all easier to recognize since they have identifiable and quantifiable skills. Aaron Schwartz saw the fundamental necessity of public access to knowledge and when he took action to liberate information from behind yet another vile maxim paywall. Afterwards, he was attacked without mercy by the (then Democratic) United States government and the administrators of MIT: self-declared "beacon of progress." Schwartz, like Berners-Lee, opted to use his considerable ability to attack the stratification of society by enabling masses to have access to knowledge. This action was taken as a declaration of war by the ruling institutions whose primary duty is to maintain social stratification by corralling resources and knowledge. When it became clear to Schwartz that his life would be mangled by the neoliberal state, he took the only remaining autonomous action he felt remained: suicide, committing the act in 2013.

The only other option for an earnest artist who refuses the aesthetics of psychopathy is to drop out of this world completely, a gesture of extreme negation that is also read as a sign of total failure at life, since such a loser must have done something to deserve it.

DEFAULT EXCLUSIONS
AND ANTI-BODIES

In addition to direct threats against the hierarchy, excluded by default is any subtle, out-of-phase development of speculative, critical potential except when it is injected dead to build immunity in the Masters-of-the-Universe body. Unpalatable, critical, marginal work is only recognized after great, anesthetizing distance, and only after it is owned and safely behind glass. As Lee Lozano put it: "Win First Don't Last/Win Last Don't Care" Lozano can't care now, so her gallery Hauser & Wirth, now "cares."

Jack Goldstein made some brilliant films and vinyl in the 1970's, but when he saw Soho heating up in the 1980's, he desperately wanted a piece of the action. The resulting paintings demonstrated all the signs of Genii at the time: big, glossy objects with icy intelligence that also look emptier and dumber as time goes by. (Our rule of thumb is to distance ourselves from people who prefer Goldstein's later paintings above his earlier film and audio work, as a matter of principal, not merely of taste.) When he wasn't received as a Genii, as he planned, he retreated dejected into the California desert, a total failure at everything except at being a good artist. (Kurismaki via his film La Havre: "My success was purely artistic.") In the last decade, Gate-Keepers have been pulling his image and work up from the deep obscurity he committed suicide to in the 1990's. His Artfacts ranking has since rocketed.

Canadian artist Rebecca Belmore was sued by her Toronto gallery because she refused to perform for them, dropping the gallery when she felt uncomfortable with how they were representing her. Faced with the threat of paying a million dollars in damages, Belmore staged a performance where she donated a work to a museum and spontaneously and publicly stated "I quit." This is funny/sad because as her wikipedia page says, her work is about "voicelessness." If an artist has already been admitted to the busy-ness field of art and refuses to perform Genii, her only remaining action is to refuse to produce art. The only remaining protest action for a reluctant artist is to get off the field and refuse the busy-ness?

Naturally we must again mention Lee Lozano who developed protests inside New York's art temples until coming to the all-too-logical conclusion that the only power position was to drop out of the art ecosystem. Forgotten for a while after her early death, Lee Lozano's work re-surfaced dramatically when Moderna Museet considered her to be sufficiently harmless — yet with enough edge to be edgy — to promote as Genii. Her old galleries still had her stuff laying around in storage, perfect!

Lygia Clark dropped out at a decisive moment, disgusted by the ecosystem. Helio Oiticica likewise decided that nothing productive happened when the euro fur-coat set strolled titillated and blasé through his works, and so he withdrew from the field, making work only for marginalized, and to him, more interesting people. Mainstream art historians don't mention his proto relational aesthetics work in a chaotic tenement in still devastated New York City because the toastmaster tastemakers were not invited, and his sharp modernism looks pretty in contrast to the Favelas in the background.

Straight, un-artistic suicide is a popular option to avoid the degradation and humiliation of social failure and resource blockage, and the surest, quickest way to drop out. It is also a fast track to canonization which may occur even if you are anonymous: a Gate-Keeper could stumble upon and see the utility of the work, in which case, watch how quickly the relatives and trustees of the deceased become smart opportunists. The inclusion of Malachi Ritscher in the 2014 Whitney Biennial smells of gasoline. One may also drop out of performative roles from various heights: the already mentioned Jack Goldstein, Jeremy Blake, Arshile Gorky, Diane Arbus, Ray Johnson, Francesca Woodman, Mike Kelly, Mark Rothko, and a very long etcetera, all carried out a final, decisive negation of their roles that cannot entirely be explained by mental illness. "This world in itself is not reasonable, that is all that can be said."[31] The production of art is an action of hope, unless the fuel for the fire is cynical sociopathy.

SURVIVAL OF THE FITTEST

The human being who is unburdened with empathy is not to be singled out as a lone gunman — the village condones and supplies arms. The village has taken the values of those at the top to be their own, pining for ascribed greatness found there. The speed, complexity and globalised world of finance covers up the behaviour of psychopaths and "even worse, makes them appear normal and even to be ideal leaders."[32] The vile maxim is driven by either psychopaths in action, or by emulation of psychopathic behaviour that has become normalized by entire ecosystems. Those who protest their lot wind up on the receiving end of the inevitable. Hannah Arendt traces the path of genius through racism: "Selected inheritance was believed to result in 'hereditary genius', and again aristocracy was held to be the natural outcome, not of politics, but of natural selection, of pure breed. To transform the whole nation into a natural aristocracy from which the best selected, the choice exemplars, would develop into the heights of geniuses and supermen, was one of the many 'ideas' which frustrated liberal intellectuals produced when they hoped to replace the old governing classes by a new 'elite' through non-political means."[33] These ideas have been picked up again.

Since social stratification is so heavily policed and systematized, anyone who appears to be able to walk freely through it looks like a supreme being. The ruthless pursuit of money is considered among the most important activities a human being can engage in because the corresponding power of agency seems supernatural. Money aligns itself as proof of superior genes, allowing those fortunate genii to float through moral, physical and class structures as mythical beings. Not only can you avoid lines, paying taxes, constant precarity of existence, and the potential of getting shot by the police for any minor civic infraction, or increasingly for no reason at all — if you need to sip cocaine laced Da Hong Pao tea out of a super-model's running shoe on a spectacular terrace overlooking central park at 4am on a Sunday, no problem!

1. E.H. Gombrich, *The Story of Art* (London: Phaidon Press, 2006), 217.

2. However even for a mathematics genius, a supportive, peaceful environment, resources, time, focus and collaboration will still be necessary to realize productive work.

3. Georg Wilhelm Friedrich Hegel, *Aesthetics: Lectures on Fine Art, Volume 1* (Oxford: Oxford University Press, 1998), 284.

4. According to figures from 2016, the World Economic Forum reports that the three EU countries where workers work the longest hours are Greece, Portugal, and Spain, smashing the "lazy" southern Europe rhetoric.

5. Hegel, "Aesthetics: Lectures on Fine Art, Volume 1" 284-285.

6. Hegel, "Aesthetics: Lectures on Fine Art, Volume 1" 284.

7. Megan Gannon, "Race Is a Social Construct Scientists Argue," *Scientific American*, February 5, 2016. https://www.scientificamerican.com/article/race-is-a-social-construct-scientists-argue.

8. Eugenics Archive, "International Eugenics" http://www.eugenicsarchive.org/html/eugenics/static/themes/25.html.

9. Maria Björkman, Sven Widmalm, "Selling eugenics: the case of Sweden," *Notes and Records of the Royal Society*. August 18, 2010. doi: 10.1098/rsnr.2010.0009.

10. Adam Smith, *The Wealth of Nations* (New York: Random House, 1937), 448.

11. Ingrid Wickelgren, "How Do You Spot a Genius?," *Scientific American*, October 18, 2012. http://blogs.scientificamerican.com/streams-of-consciousness/2012/10/18/how-do-you-spot-a-genius.

12. Joshua W Buckholtz, Michael T Treadway, Ronald L Cowan, Neil D Woodward, Stephen D Benning, Rui Li, M Sib Ansari, Ronald M Baldwin, Ashley N Schwartzman, Evan S Shelby, Clarence E Smith, David Cole, Robert M Kessler & David H Zald, "Mesolimbic dopamine reward system hypersensitivity in individuals with psychopathic traits," *Nature Neuroscience* 13, 419–421 (2010) doi: 10.1038/nn.2510.

13. McHoskey, J. W., Worzel, W., & Szyarto, C. "Machiavellianism and psychopathy" *Journal of Personality and Social Psychology*, 74(1), 192-210 (1998) doi: http://dx.doi.org/10.1037/0022-3514.74.1.192.

14. Kevin Dutton, *The Wisdom of Psychopaths* (New York: Doubleday, 2012).

15. Kevin Dutten, "Psychopaths at the Office?" *Scientific American Mind*, (December 19, 2012) doi: 10.1038/scientificamericanmind0113-36.

16. Michael W. Kraus, Stéphane Côté, and Dacher Keltner, "Social Class, Contextualism, and Empathic Accuracy" *Association for Psychological Science* Vol 21, Issue 11 (October 25, 2010): 1716-1723. https://doi.org/10.1177/0956797610387613.

17. Charles McGrath, "Compromising Dolls and Pink Panthers," *New York Times*, December 26, 2012. http://www.nytimes.com/2012/12/27/arts/design/a-new-novel-an-art-show-and-book-by-bjarne-melgaard.html.

18. Marion Charret-Del Bove and Françoise Palleau-Papin, "Vanessa Place: An Interview In Paris," *Transatlantica, American Studies Journal*, June 7, 2012. transatlantica.revues.org/5724.

19. Law and Order Wiki, "Vanessa Place" http://lawandorder.wikia.com/wiki/Vanessa_Place.

20. The sway of psychopaths, or at least the aesthetics of psychopathy, moves the left as easily as it moves the right, no one is immune because several tailor made strategies are used. The left promotes the cruelty of business as usual, and the right promotes more bigotry.

21. Guy Debord, *Society of the Spectacle* (Detroit, Black and Red Press, 1977), 12.

22. Hannah Arendt, "Race-Thinking Before Racism," *The Review of Politics*, Vol. 6, No. 1 (January 1944): 51. http://www.jstor.org/stable/1404080.

23. MIT seeking "internationally recognized" creative producer, September 2016: http://act.mit.edu/wp-content/uploads/2016/10/ACT_Tenured-Associate-or-Full-Professor-Job-Description.pdf.

24. Robert F. Bornstein, "Exposure and affect: Overview and meta-analysis of research, 1968-1987," *Psychological Bulletin* 106 (1989): 265–289. doi: http://psycnet.apa.org/record/1990-00422-001?doi=1.

25. Matthew J. Salganik, Peter Sheridan Dodds, Duncan J. Watts, "Experimental Study of Inequality and Unpredictability in an Artificial Cultural Market," *Science* 10, Vol. 311, Issue 5762 (February 10, 2006): 854-856. doi: 10.1126/science.1121066.

26. Sadie Gennis, "Help! I'm in Love with a TV Psychopath," *Today's News*, March 10, 2013. http://www.tvguide.com/news/following-tv-psychopath-love-1062532.

27. perifericbiennale, "Interview with Marek Claassen, the director of artfacts.net," *perifericbiennale*, October 20, 2008. https://perifericbiennial.wordpress.com/2008/10/20/interview-with-with-marek-claassen-the-director-of-artfactsnet.

28. All Marek Claassen quotes, if not footnoted, were found in artfacts.net

29. Rafael Rozendaal, "Success is Exponential," *New Rafael blog*. http://www.newrafael.com/success-is-exponential.

30. Arthur Schopenhauer, *Parerga and Paralipomena: A Collection of Philosophical Essays* (New York, Cosimo, 2007), 86.

31. Albert Camus, *The Myth of Sisyphus and Other Essays* (New York City, Knopf Doubleday Publishing Group, 1991), 21.

32. Clive R. Boddy, "The Corporate Psychopaths Theory of the Global Financial Crisis," *Journal of Business Ethics*, 102 (2) (2011): 255-259. doi: 10.1007/s10551-011-0810-4.

33. Hannah Arendt, "Race-Thinking Before Racism," *The Review of Politics*, Vol. 6, No. 1 (January, 1944): 66.

AGENCY
AND TASTE

Judgement, if we follow Hannah Arendt, is an essential human faculty, opposed to morality, that allows us, as individuals, to distinguish right from wrong. So-called common sense and its moral basis must be discarded by a being aspiring to supra-moral, internal equilibrium. One must follow *deines eigenes Weg*, to follow one's own path, no banisters, and step away from the framed view. She took from Nietzsche the lost hand-rails in Zarathustra: "Have not all hand-rails [banisters] and foot-bridges fallen into the water?"[1] Nietzsche understood Kant's insistence to follow *deines eigenes Weg*: to have an engaged internal dialogue at every step and to act in a way consistent with one's own compass.

Taste is disguised as a naturalistic judgement of fact, as though it could be universal, rational, and follow objective rules. Arendt instead made a case via Kant that judgement could be evidence of a basic, supra-moral, human faculty that can be applied to larger social issues such as exploitation and murder as well as smaller things such as a painting. While still insightful even today, there are several deep problems in this path, and we aim to unpack some of them here.

MORALITY

Morality is radically flaky. Morality is a weak substitute for thinking. Morality only accidentally touches truth and justice. Morality, especially when encoded into law, replaces empathy with guilt. Morality is an unreliable guide for the human being who wishes to do more good than harm. Arendt argues that it is impossible to reconcile morality with a universal rule, instead one must use "an independent human faculty, unsupported by law and public opinion, that judges anew in full spontaneity every deed and intent whenever the occasion arises."[2]

Morality and law (its codification) were invented in order to control those in the population who were incapable or unwilling to judge for themselves. Arendt: "those few whose nature, the nature of their souls, lets them see the truth, don't need any oblation, any 'Thou Shalt — or else,' because what matters is self-evident. And since those who don't see the truth can't be convinced by arguments, some means has to be found to make them behave, to force them to act, without being convinced — as though they, too, had 'seen.'"[3] The necessities of religion, morality, law — and in art: taste — are useful to those who cannot see, think, and judge for themselves based on internal equilibrium, lived experience, and evidence at hand, without bannisters.

Arendt found in Kant and Nietzsche an assertion that ethical balance during extreme situations without moral precedent rests on a potential faculty of judgement. This faculty is needed again and again in situations that are historically unique and nuanced where evil appears in its infinite forms. One finds the patterns in human horror by drawing on one's faculty of judgement, if something like this exists.

AGENCY JUDGEMENT

Arendt argued that instead of following morality unthinking, we need a concept of judgement that is based on something else. Sound judgement could be within the independence found in a mix of empirical and speculative reason combined with just the right amount of intuition. While it is impossible to judge without cognitive bias, free from all structures, it is possible to become semi-aware of one's position in relation to everyone else's, by training an *enlarged mentality*. What are the characteristics needed for the equilibrium in judgement that could produce a more ethical, equitable society than morality has proven capable? Adaptable, oscillating and insightful: agency and selfless curiosity are only the beginning. One does not simply follow or oppose moral, conformist-realist judgment by default, instead, one oscillates with counterfactual agility, internal chemistry, and some *pure reason* that is not at all pure. Judgement based on critical, thoughtful agency could be the base of just action, especially when tempered by the intuitive spirit that distinguishes human beings from thoughtless automaton reacting purely by program, reacting obediently to the vacuous brutality of law and order. There is a crucial difference between forced obedience and free consent to an authority, retaining the option to withdraw consent if necessary.

Arendt's striking thoughts on judgement were made during her reflections on the Eichman trial, so let's follow her reasoning there.[1] Rather than concentrating on the specific victim and perpetrator, Arendt used the trial to map a previously uncharted human condition precisely in order to recognize it when evil inevitably occurs again, in all its varieties, in the future. Judith Butler's review of Arendt in the London Book Review described it thusly: "What happened to the Jewish people under Hitler should not be seen as exceptional but as exemplary of a certain way of managing minority populations."[4] It is folly to search for or claim equivalents in manifestations of horror. Arendt instead was searching for how the roots of anti-Semitism could be expanded to understand the too-common process of devaluating human life.

Arendt argues that the replacement of one cluster of morals for another, relatively rapidly, (spanning less than a generation) in the case of the National Socialist Workers Party, made painfully clear, forever, that the morals constructed by society are rubbish, especially when they are expressed in law. German society changed from a society that recognized the basic humanity and rights of all its citizens to one that singled out, tortured and murdered millions of its own citizens, and then it changed again to a society that recognized the basic rights of its citizens again. German bourgeoisie classes adjusted seemingly effortlessly to the predominant morals before, during and after the Third Reich. High-society parties thrown by the German bourgeoisie during the Third Reich were epic, completely void of conscience, and continued not long after the surrender. To be well-adjusted was the primary objective for German bourgeoisie to stay on top of the social hierarchy, even during the extreme actions of othering and then murdering one's own brothers and sisters. While the othering and murder of foreign "savages" was already acceptable to the average European, it took some effort to sell the murder of those closer to home.

SELLING MURDER

Our ability to navigate right action depends on our capacity to make judgments, outside of morality. For example, murder is normally bad taste: murder is not always illegal, but it likely leaves a bad taste in one's mouth, therefore most people make a personal judgement against it, nearly universally, especially with one's own hands. Thus, murder, (and violence, theft and exploitation) has to be marketed and sold to citizens as the moral act. In colonialism for example, it must be established that *not* to murder is immoral, or at least inconvenient due to invented moral intervention. This is where Arendt's search for a faculty of judgment breaks down: looking for universals of judgement suffer too many worldwide exceptions that are so easily made palatable and then legal by special interests. Simone de Beauvoir is not generous towards the classes who condone horror: "We are free to define our conditions, and thus free to set value. The well-adjusted forget or supress this fact."[5]

Legal arguments are produced and trotted out in congress, at the UN, and NATO, and the war crimes tribunal in the Hague, and the U.S. courts and the media, etc. thus allowing horror to fit a "civilized" moral framework. Murder (and violence, theft and exploitation) is fully moral, under the right circumstances. The fact that murder leaves a bad taste in one's mouth does not influence greater morality as demonstrated by state murder followed by great melancholic gestures of pure self-interest. This tradition has continued undeterred as we see in the full, murderous occupations of Iraq, Afghanistan, Syria, and Palestine. We see murder marketed as moral, and sold as the fully legal drone strikes and bombings of various Pakistani, Libyan, and Yemeni villages. We see racial colonialism (to use bell hooks' terminology) in the on-going police murders of black, brown and working class people in various public and private situations that are deemed lawful again and again by the courts and juries of the United States, backed by a thinning majority of voters who have been sold the wretched morality of murder. The number of military and police cases of post-traumatic stress disorder may indicate that the majority of those who actually commit the murders with their hands, and see mutilated bodies close-up, find the act tasteless, even when they delude themselves that murder is moral. Only actual psychopaths are undisturbed by murder, and they swell the ranks of police, military, and mercenary contractors even though clinical psychopaths are an extreme minority in society as a whole.

Selling murder is difficult, and intellectuals have taken great pains to do so at the service of power. Race-thinking developed into full racism, enabling a "civilized" population to imagine they were simply living the inevitable hierarchy of racial aristocracy. In a short paper called "Race Thinking Before Racism" Arendt traced racism through European imperialism, locating it firmly in its use as a tool for an exclusive caste of foreign rule in the colonies that Benjamin Disraeli argued was according to "the aristocracy of nature."[6] While Disraeli sold Jewish genealogy as an aristocratic asset, Arendt noted that concepts such as the "true nobility" of advanced races would fan the embers of social Anti-Semitism into the raging flames of official "Jew-hating as a political weapon."[7] We see countless examples today of the political convenience of selling murder (and violence, theft and exploitation) to the "rational" and moral citizens of many nations, including the rising return of anti-Semitism as a political weapon.

MURDER IS MURDER

For Arendt, murder by turning against, othering, a nation state's own people, crossed a line unimaginable until then. The collapse of morality was total when all classes in Germany accepted, condoned, and systematized the murder of their own fellow citizens. Colonial genocide fit within the moral structures of European societies because colonizing nation states already identified the colonized as *other*, less than human, and therefore morally and then legally murderable.

Arendt's admiration of Winston Churchill who she called "the greatest statesman, thus far, of our century"[8] is a strange footnote in morality studies. Churchill's open racism, views on eugenics, [9] his twisted advocacy of chemical weapons,[10] his policies that purposely, brutally starved to death millions of people in India, and his advocacy of race supremacy generally showed that his morality was almost interchangeable with Hitler. Because mass murder of an *other* is consistent with the colonial project, it is thus consistently moral and thus not a moment of moral collapse. We understand Arendt's text as a call to expand the human faculty of judgement to cover vile acts that are nevertheless considered moral. Why then, was she unable to enlarge her own mentality to judge Churchill's extreme racism in parallel with Nazi racism and anti-Semitism? Winston Churchill was a vile, murderous racist if we judge him from a basic factual perspective. However, if we look at him as an English "statesman," who advocated murderously for his own people, then he appears to be great, moral, tasteful and also, fully within legal bounds. Where was Arendt's *amor mundi* in this formulation?

TASTE AND JUDGMENT

We do not suggest that Arendt implied a direct link between morality and aesthetics. However, aesthetics trains consensus, consent, and art sells morality. Art and taste are historically intertwined, and taste is learned, unthinking obedience. Most individuals are unable to understand or conceptualize where their own taste comes from, and thus the moral structure that determines taste remains an invisible, powerful force that shapes the world. Taste changes, like morality, sometimes suddenly and radically, rendering their utility clearly. The value of both morality and taste is anthropological: they describe a zeitgeist, as in detached, cultural studies, but cannot be used as lodestar to navigate against horror or disgust.

Judgement without bannisters is the attempt to be conscious of habitus. While it is impossible to fully escape one's environment, education, background, class and thus taste, it is possible to be semi-conscious of it via active re-evaluation, and thus, to decide purposefully to take responsibility. To take responsibility for one's own tastes does not mean that one must rail against the tastes of one's habitus by default, as in the history of the avant-guard. The avant-guard is futilely pegged to morality and normality, opposing it by reflex, and thus forced forever to follow it obediently in blind disobedience. (This is related to our earlier formulation that Satanism is still Christianity.) Instead of such a reaction, one must judge for one's self, during every single event, based on the very best of one's ability to understand evidence gathered by active data seeking, combined with the self-awareness and empathy that comes from the realization that a judgement could be mistaken. One's judgment will thus fall in and out of sync with the current morality, taste, and law, oscillating with established fact and new information.

TASTE AS NORMALIZED
CULTURAL SUPERIORITY

Taste, and its opposite, disgust, (both oral-based), add to naturalistic-appearing discourses employed to normalize cultural superiority. Researchers Kelly and Morar wrote about disgust as a social reflex. "Disgust has been brought to bear on a variety of social issues, in some cases providing the motivation to comply with certain social norms and to punish those who violate them, and in other cases providing the motivation to avoid interactions with members of other social groups, who engage in different practices and subscribe to a different set of values and norms."[11] The same physical response to avoid contaminated food and poison is transferred to other people and their cultural norms such as ritual, art, fashion, and behavioral norms, as well as food. This leap is too large to be rational, except if we consider its utility for social control.

ART AND NORMALITY

K-Hole: "You've been working so hard at being precise that the micro-logic of your decisions is only apparent to an ever-narrowing circle of friends. You may be the world's foremost expert in Religious Dance of Melanesia. But after you graduate, you realize no one gives a fuck besides your PhD advisor. This is the story of the world's most exasperated Subway employee."[12] Normcore is elite, conformist-realist camouflage. Young masters of the universe, and their dogged administrators, pass through the city indistinguishable from middle-American mall mainstream, rule goes unnoticed. You have two choices: get well-adjusted to the morality and taste of a particular class, or else end up pulverized, laboring unfulfilled, (K-Hole suggests in fast food, positioned near the bottom of the neoliberal food-chain.) The ruling class remains so by selling norms, products, and ideas to the masses. The masters of the universe delights in covering up class all together: everything in neoliberalism is a meritocracy! Normcore is (was) a highly-developed form of conformist-realism, demanding adherence to taste at the expense of any potential faculty of judgment, because that is where victory lies: in the supply chains of our current normality.

JUDGMENT AND CURATORS

A potential human faculty of judgement is completely different than the gate-keeping action of art's gate-keepers who are unwilling or unable to make judgments based on any criteria other than the fickle tastes of trend cycles locked into taste. While the stakes and gravity are higher and graver in political policy engraved as law, we see the same default judgment process infused throughout the system. In art we sketched a term that shadows the psychopathy of morality: Genii-Aesthetics, the formalized law of convenient, conformist selection disguised as natural selection.

If a gate-keeper is mentally capable of judgment without bannisters, and one particular judgment runs into moral conflict with their assigned role, they must set it aside for the sake of their masters, which they justify to themselves is the greater good. Being well-adjusted and obedient to current morality confers the material and progenitive advantages of self-preservation. For example, if a gate-keeper notices something inconvenient then the gate-keeper must put aside such distasteful facts and information. A curator for example, when arranging timely, show-must-go-on fairs, must follow current morality and taste and thus please the trustees of the institution they work for, and appease the masters-of-the-universe who demand to see themselves reflected in all their institutions. One of the intellectual founders of neoliberalism, F. A. Hayek wrote in 1949 that the power and influence of experts such as scientists and researchers has been usurped by the general intellectual whose role is to carefully select information to disseminate on behalf of the institution. The intellectual therefore "is neither that of the original thinker nor that of the scholar or expert in a particular field of thought. The typical intellectual need be neither: he (sic) need not possess special knowledge of anything in particular, nor need he even be particularly intelligent, to perform his role as intermediary in the spreading of ideas."[13] This is a further rightward development of Gramsci's formulation in the Prison Notebooks of the "traditional intellectual" who is bound to the institutions of hegemony, despite claims of disinterest and autonomy. Plehwe and Walpen noted "Hayek observes the rapid spread of such institutions breeding intellectuals (and not experts) such as universities, foundations, institutes, editors and other knowledge spreading organizations such as journals, etc. as a highly important location to spread neoliberal ideas.[14] According to Hayek the role of intellectuals as knowledge filters and disseminators, as 'second hand dealers in ideas' must be swayed from socialism towards neoliberalism.[15] Whether or not a curator understands or recognizes their true role in art institutions, where the boards are unambiguously comprised of the leaders of industry, finance and tech, does not matter: they perform with great precision.

Part of the role of the curator, especially of the flagship institutions of the world's power-centers, is to somehow appease even hostile elements among the more vocal within the res-publica, while hard-selling current morality. The curator must balance demands made by socially progressive groups such as anti-racism and anti-homophobia for example, at least while power ascendant, with more conservative social voices who pine for what is already known to be "morally right" according to what is sadly confused for natural selection. Few gate-keepers these days will publically declare that they are nationalist, racist, and misogynist, however, they typically follow the taste to place African, Asian and European art and artists on unequal terms, male and female artists on unequal terms, or foreign and national artists on unequal terms, art from lower classes on unequal terms with ruling classes, and so on. Curators respond with sudden changes of heart and token admissions when outrage against obvious bias becomes too rowdy, but without disturbing the previous order to any great degree. This is why during the Obama administration there were suddenly more black and brown people promoted in culture, but this peaked and began its decline after Trump. Even small, token signs of resistance to comply is a punishable offence, witness the sudden dismissals of Helen Molesworth and Laura Raicovich, and other, less visible exclusions of threatening curators, directors, and writers. In order to stay on top and give an appearance of meritocracy and otherwise further the neoliberal ideals of the institutions they belong to, Gate-Keepers must carefully blend in with local norms. Such contorted balance between opposing local social pressures is essential to advance the relentless goal of the institution: neoliberalism.[16]

DIFFERENCES OF TASTE

There are differences of taste at the top: the worst among them cannot even tolerate feigned institutional criticism or any illusion of freedom in art. The more fascist and bureaucratic among the Masters-of-the-Universe and their Gate-Keepers are so limited they insist on being surrounded un-ironically by celebratory kitsch. Trump, Putin and Berlusconi types prefer the vulgarity of neo-Roman/neo-harem interiors to any clean, sober design because even the slightest references to the social reform inherent somewhere hidden deep within modernism is detected like pigs sniff out truffles in the forest underbrush. However, taste runs in clusters, depending on habitus, and functions in exactly the same way. Wall Street hedge fund manager Steven Mnunchin, a Trump appointee, is the son of Robert Mnunchin, uptown Manhattan art dealer. Ivanka Trump was photographed in her drawing room with expensive, edgy, bullet-hole shaped Nate Lowman art behind her, probably symbolizing the hole where their empathy is hurled. High-brow, low brow, middle brow: unthinking adherents to each respective brow-rank toss herbicide on weeds of thought sprouting amidst the perfectly manicured uniformity of the green lawns of culture. Eclectic, uneducated, and vulgar tastes follow the unthinking judgment of group-cohesiveness in the same way that more "sophisticated" taste does. The market revels in variety.

GROUP-THINK VS. JUDGEMENT

Group-think is a mind-set that allows (W.E.I.R.D.) individuals to completely evade all responsibility for judgement. Many studies confirm the presence of group-think behaviour such as the Asch conformity experiments from the 1950's. Our favourite study of the phenomenon is the *strawberry yoghurt study* where college students were asked to identify food in a blind taste test. Researchers planted people who tasted strawberry yogurt and said it tasted like vanilla, and 80% of the time the unknowing subject conformed to the group opinion although they knew what they tasted was unmistakably strawberry yogurt.

The part that gives us hope in these studies is the fact that conforming individuals knew deep down that they tasted strawberry, and even admitted it after the study was over. The darkest hour is when an individual cannot even detect that they are eating strawberry, so sure of the correctness of peer-pressure morality – unable to stand cognitive dissonance, they alter their own taste buds with the awesome power of their inner conformist – they eat strawberry and they taste vanilla, banana, or even garlic! Group dynamics produces an *illusion of invulnerability*, that is, inflated certainty that the right decision has been made. An individual defeated by a wildberry, and the entire ecosystem wallows in delusion.

A HUMAN FACULTY FOR CONFORMITY

The Strawberry Yoghurt Study leads us to suggest that human beings have a universal faculty for conformity. Somewhere deep within people, there is a switch that flicks off and on telling one to listen to the group, and disregard one's own faculty of reason. We could call this faculty the Vanilla Switch.

Simon de Beauvoir described lack of freedom as a person submitting to the world as it stands. "This means that the world in which he lives is a serious world, since the characteristic of the spirit of seriousness is to consider values as ready-made things."[7] Borrowing from Hegel, Kierkegaard and Nietzsche, de Beauvoir establishes a hierarchy of unfreedom. Through life, different types of people react to the horror and responsibility of absolute freedom. The sub-man follows values blindly without question, the serious man is handicapped by allegiance to "higher" values, the nihilist opts out and values nothing, the adventurer (today's neoliberal player) games the system for the sake of adventure, and the passionate man selfishly exploits everyone. She finally suggests the possibility of freedom: "To will oneself free is also to will others free."[18] The neoliberal ecosystem wills and then legislates unfreedom.

THE LAWS OF JANTE

Norwegian Janteloven is a strange, related phenomenon: it is hyggelig, (cozy), to be well-adjusted to majority opinion! Janteloven promotes nationalist group harmony as a cover-up to buttress the usual hegemonic structures. Hostility towards difference takes the form of passive-aggressive exclusion via Janteloven that is implemented across all social classes as a hands-off, efficient form for a self-policing population. The concept of Janteloven comes from the Danish-Norwegian author Aksel Sandemose in his 1933 book *En flyktning krysser sitt spor*. He captured the oppressive spirit of social adhesion so closely that Janteloven is now in the general vocabulary of Scandinavia.

Here are a few key Laws of Jante, the unspoken moral operative:

You're not to think you are smarter than us. You're not to convince yourself that you are better than us. You're not to think you are good at anything. You're not to laugh at us. You're not to think anyone cares about you. You're not to think you can teach us anything.

Who is the *us* and who is the *you* in this law? In the case of a foreigner, person of color, and person of nonconforming gender in Norway, this *you* is easy to identify and developed with oppression in mind. However, in the case of a white, heterosexual, male Norwegian, who is *you* and who is *us*? *You* is anyone who judges and acts as an individual using judgment without bannisters. *You* is anyone who decides that a particular majority taste is disgusting.

Janteloven is expressed in the art ecosystem too: Norway's hippest, taste-making, popular art gallery is fittingly called Standard, and shows mostly mute, vacant work of self-censuring formalism, completely drained of any threatening content and difference. Standard is unthreatening and irritatingly worse than silence. The Ambiguism[19] on display here is feigned enigma that clearly promotes mid-range consensus. While it is sometimes argued internally that Janteloven is the reason that there are no 3 Michelin starred restaurants in Norway, in fact, Janteloven is used by Norway to promote itself as the most equal society on earth. It is dark comedy: "more-equal" does not mean "equal", and in fact, Norway is in the top 5 among industrial nations with the fastest increase of social inequality.[20] Despite a rhetoric of equality, the Norwegians have not even shed their clownish royals. In Norway, winner takes most instead of winner takes all, but the ruling classes are slowly grinding that away too. The Norwegians are seeing how peers in other countries behave, and they are beginning to conform to the international moral standard that has outgrown even the quaintly oppressive local Janteloven. Norway is all aboard the neoliberal train, conforming to its nation-state peers, practicing Janteloven on itself.

CLASS TASTE

While royal courts no longer influence taste and courtesy, manners were handed down from there to class and national affiliations, and to consumer preferences stratified between classes. Form is confused with function in its mandate of control: any fork will function with a salad and any cut of clothing will shelter against the elements, unless you ask a courtier, or a 5th grader in the school lunch-room looking around desperately to fit in. Lower classes mirror ruling class tastes, altering or misinterpreting slightly. "Superior taste" is also developed and maintained by the ruling class with careful, *curated*, vital appropriations from the lower classes. The upper class loves to mix earthy habits with their own refinements and thus maintain distinction while maintaining some fun dynamics. The King of Norway wears an old, battered, farmer jacket when he holidays in the countryside. There are photos of Ben Bernanke sporting a baseball cap on his days off of his old job. Silicon valley moguls wear hoodies and jeans all the time: they have become so powerful by exploiting the labor and attention spans of the masses, that they realize tailored, luxury suits would be tasteless, and so they wear the attire to blend in with their most avid follower: the college student. (Their jumbo-salaried corporate lawyers and capital hill lobbyists however, still sport suits.) It is "bad taste" for the upper-class and cultural elite to adopt, wholesale, lower-class tastes, but this is, in fact, good taste when rules for how to pull it off are strictly followed.

TRANSGRESSION = GOOD TASTE

It is important to stress that for the past one hundred or so years, since at least Charles Baudelaire wrote "...give them only carefully selected garbage,"[21] having "bad taste" is a sign of progress, and thus "bad taste" became "good taste" quite some time ago when an elite among the bourgeoisie picked up on how titillating and tasteful it was to lightly violate bourgeoisie taste. By appropriating elements of working class or struggling college student taste for example, by appropriating black vernacular language, or by violating out-dated bourgeoisie taste and morality. Cutting edge demonstrates bad-good edginess to set themselves ever-so-slightly apart from their less competitive peers. Bad-good taste is not evidence of seeing, thinking and judging for oneself using actual thought without bannisters. How to have bad-good taste is an interesting construction because it must carefully break meticulously selected tastes and morals that have been earmarked for transgression. One mustn't be too white. Carefully groomed bad-good taste cannot just pick any taste or moral to break, it must break tastes and morals that are already out dated, prudish, or too white.

Let's look at Normcore again. Normcore seeks the bland anonymity of mass fashion as a way of not standing out in the crowd. Simmel wrote more than a century ago that when a ruling class is made of few, self-preservation is more important than self-expression: "...the Venetian nobili had no fashion since they were all required by a specific law to wear black, so as not to make their small numbers all too obvious to the lower strata. Here there was no fashion since the other constitutive element was missing, because differentiation from their social inferiors was to be deliberately avoided."[22] Normcore emphasizes that the elite are invisibly circulating among us, blending in (like John Carpenter's film "They Live,") with frumpy, unsophisticated, pathetic, off-the-rack, Polo, Patagonia, New Balance and Nike: the "tasteless" accoutrements of low/middle culture from suburban wastelands that become the latest high culture symbols for tiny, elite (and yearning) circles roaming Kreuzkölln, Williamsburg, Peckham, Yaletown, etc. The previously mentioned Silicon Valley elite are the vampire gods of extreme Normcore, feeding on the blood of the struggling precariat while looking as frumpy (and thus unthreatening) as possible.

Like King Midas, Duchamp, Warhol, and Richard Prince, high culture needs only to tap low culture to convert it into gold.[23] The more difficult and challenging it is to tell the classes apart, the easier it is to play the game with impunity.[24] Adapting lower-class tastes is accessorizing with the trophy bones of defeated enemies. Simmel described it thusly: "...on the one hand, fashion signifies a union with those of the same status, the uniformity of a social circle characterized by it, and, in so doing, the closure of this group against those standing in a lower position which the higher group characterizes as not belonging to it."[25] Violation of out-dated bourgeois morals is the perfect disguise for the ruling-classes, since it simply cannot be criticized. All criticism of the violation of out-dated bourgeois morals and taste are deflected with reflex accusations that such a critic is conservative, out dated, uncool, dusty, and therefore is easily identified as not one of them and thus excluded by design.

INDIVIDUALISM AND NEOLIBERALISM

What Arendt could almost be advocating in her thesis on judgement is the responsibility as an individual. This very nearly sounds like the root advocacy of individualist neoliberalism. Agency judgement places overwhelming responsibility on the shoulders of the over-burdened, atomized person. The ability to judge independently, and the power and agency to act upon the results, especially if not in accord with the larger group, demands an *Übermensch*. And this exact character is idealized and worshiped in neoliberalism. Silicon Valley is bursting with individualist non-conformists who have forged bold business models by shattering morality and taste, and gotten so unimaginably rich, that they are producing culture and society in their own perverse image, making reality out of Ayn Rand's dreams of The Fountainhead. The current *Übermensch* is the entrepreneurial "disruptor" who produces unicorn "revolutions" of consumer swarming patterns.

However, this is where we need to reconsider Arendt's suggestion of an *enlarged mentality*. The individual who judges without a bannister does so by imagining themselves in the space of another human being and thus cannot look at people in competition as other, the default relationship in neoliberalism. When accused by Gershom Scholem of having no love of the Jewish people Arendt famously responded: "I have never in my life 'loved' any people or collective – neither the German people, nor the French, nor the American, nor the working class or anything of that sort. I indeed love 'only' my friends and the only kind of love I know of and believe in is the love of persons."[26] Arendt's love for individuals could almost pass for Milton Friedman's love for individualism. However, Friedman's declaration that "freedom is a rare and delicate plant," offers little hope either for the average individual, or for actual rare and delicate plants. Arendt's love is specific, for specific individuals that she knows, whereas Friedman's is pure abstraction, speculation that will never come true.

By loving people instead of an abstract concept of a folk, (or worse, a concept of "progress,") Arendt describes a humanism that is about voluntary individual connections that expand to potentially everyone without resorting to dehumanizing broad strokes. Judgment is rendered based on an extension of the self to a neighbour who is also an individual. An individual does not allow oneself to be overwhelmed by the hive. An individual is connected to other individuals by consciously imagining that they are joined voluntarily, and could potentially love each other individually. In this way, a real community is formed by bonds of empowerment, made up of individuals who have agency and choose to be together instead of being coerced into a tribe mentality. Nationalist abstraction is the location where emotion is manipulated by *Übermensch*, entrepreneurs, demagogues, and other psychopaths roaming the earth. Arendt's brilliant formulation is made more painful but not less true when she could not expand it to her views of Churchill, the murderous and vile racist. India was simply too far away from her Upper-West Side Manhattan co-op apartment for her to realize that there are individuals living there too, to be loved.

1. Peter Marden, *The Authoritarian Interlude: Democracy, Values and the Politics of Hubris* (New York, Routledge, 2015), 217.

2. Hannah Arendt, "Responsibility and Judgment: Personal Responsibility under Dictatorship," *The Listener* (1964): 187.

3. Hannah Arendt, *Responsibility and Judgment* (New York: Schocken Books, 2003), 88.
It is not our intention to compare suffering, but following Arendt, to make sense of the human condition, to find patterns in evil as it reappears in different forms.

4. Judith Butler, "I Merely Belong to Them," *London Book Review*, vol. 29 no. 9 (10 May 2007)

5. Simon de Beauvoir, "The Ethics of Ambiguity," part II. https://www.marxists.org/reference/subject/ethics/de-beauvoir/ambiguity/cho2.htm.

6. Hannah Arendt, "Race Thinking before Racism," *The Review of Politics*, Vol. 6, No. 1 (January 1944): 52.

7. Hannah Arendt, "Race Thinking before Racism," *The Review of Politics*, Vol. 6, No. 1 (January 1944): 52.

8. Hannah Arendt, "Some Questions of Moral Phylosophy," *Social Research*, Vol. 61, No. 4, Sixtieth Anniversary 1934-1994 (Winter 1994): 739.

9. Winston Churchill told the Palestine Royal Commission in 1937 "I do not admit for instance, that a great wrong has been done to the Red Indians of America or the black people of Australia. I do not admit that a wrong has been done to these people by the fact that a stronger race, a higher-grade race, a more worldly wise race to put it that way, has come in and taken their place."

10. Giles Milton, "Winston Churchill's shocking use of chemical weapons," *The Guardian*, September 1, 2013. https://www.theguardian.com/world/shortcuts/2013/sep/01/winston-churchill-shocking-use-chemical-weapons.
Winston Churchill: "I am strongly in favour of using poisoned gas against uncivilised tribes."

11. Daniel Kelly and Nicolae Morar, "Against the Yuck Factor: On the Ideal Role of Disgust in Society," *Utilitas Journal*, Cambridge University Press. Vol. 26, Issue 2. (June, 2014)

12. K-Hole, "Youth. A Report on Freedom," http://khole.net/dl?v=4.

13. F. A. Hayek, "The Intellectuals and Socialism," *University of Chicago Law Review* (1949): 418.

14. Dieter Plehwe, Bernhard Walpen, Gisela Neunhoffer, Eds., *Neoliberal Hegemony: A Global Critique* (London: Routledge, 2006).

15. Plehwe, Walpen, Neunhoffer, *Neoliberal Hegemony: A Global Critique*, 32.

16. Gate-Keepers rarely acknowledge the fact that, for example, only 5% of all art being shown in museums in the United States in 2013 was produced by women. Gate-keepers usually ignore race/culture, for example the Whitney Museum opened its new building in 2015 with a show about "America" with 79.5% white artists, or that any non-western artist shown at institutions in Europe are filed under a othering, "orientalism" category such as "Arab Spring", etc. A Gate-Keeper will almost never hesitate to show artists collected by the trustees and boards of the museums they are employed by, and will even become insulted if questioned about this standard practice. A Gate-Keeper will only select members of lower classes if they are conveniently exotic, and/or politely demonstrate token "meritocracy" and/or enlightened liberal "democracy", but only in limited numbers, and always with a dismissive addendum that leaves such strategic inclusions in the margins.

17. Simon de Beauvoir, "The Ethics of Ambiguity," part II. https://www.marxists.org/reference/subject/ethics/de-beauvoir/ambiguity/cho2.htm.

18. de Beauvoir, "The Ethics of Ambiguity"

19. See the essay "Ambiguism" in this book.

20. Statistics Norway, "Wealth distribution in Norway. Evidence from a new register-based data source," November 22, 2012. https://www.ssb.no/en/inntekt-og-forbruk/artikler-og-publikasjoner/wealth-distribution-in-norway.

21. David DiMeo, *Committed to Disillusion: Activist Writers in Egypt from the 1950s to the 1980s* (Cairo/New York, The American University in Cairo Press, 2016), 30.

22. Georg Simmel, *On Culture* (London: SAGE Publications Ltd, 1997), 192.

23. The outrage some artists like Richard Prince demonstrated post-Trump is a taste-based issue: the elite of the left prefer quiet, veiled exploitation, and the elite of the right prefer boastful, naturalized gestures of "winning."

24. This is why Trump's vulgarity whistled the winning tune with lower class voters, while upper class voters heard the elite dog whistle directed towards them.

25. Simmel, *On Culture*, 189.

26. Judith Butler, "I merely belong to them," *London Review of Books* Vol. 29 No. 9 (May 10, 2007).

JUDGEMENT BY TING, DING AND ÞING

When we look at prizes for art, architecture and books, grant awards, professor appointments, biennial lists, and other acts of professional judgement of art by jury, the most visible and thus the most scrutinized face of this process are those who win the prizes, and get the shows and appointments. What is not scrutinized often enough are the judges themselves and less so, the appointers of judges. Who chooses the jury and the judge? What is the mechanism and the criteria for choosing judges?

The selection of the jury will — lest we forget — determine, by definition, the outcome of any juried event. Therefore, the selection of the jury itself is the most powerful act in the process that sets into motion limited results. The selection of a jury to judge something in the art ecosystem is not challenged enough: but in a court of law, jury selection is an essential first battle in a jury trial.[1]

The selection of a culture jury is mainly done in the following manners:

1. Heredity: some spots are simply passed down, no questions asked.

2. Previous winners of the same concourse: once one has been chosen, one is somehow qualified to choose in return: naturally by natural selection, ensuring a clear, unbroken, ideological line.

3. Political appointment: strategic allies of an interested person or body are chosen, tapped on the shoulder, to insure a clear, unbroken, ideological line.

4. Inside election: a governing body such as a collegium, a board, or a papal conclave conducts a small, unheralded election amongst themselves to determine who will best represent the will of that body, ensuring a clear, unbroken, ideological line.

In every one of these cases, the end result is the same: naturalization, normalization, self-propagation, and the entropy of forced competition. Councils, juries, committees and "common-sense" bodies, selected or "elected," appear to judge with free agency, however, they are expected to select according to prejudice. A legal jury is a body of people sworn to render a judgement of fact, where a judge is meant to render a judgement of law. This is rather against the usual function of a jury: it will be more likely to judge in line with generally accepted values of a society or group within that society. "Generally accepted values" overlap fact and allow truth only by coincidence, not by design. A jury more often than not simply repeats structures with rhetoric disguised as natural phenomena, justified by the empty performance of free agency, in the name of "quality" or one of many other vague words used to imply impartiality.

On occasion, shifting political winds enable the take-over of boards and juries. In culture, we last saw this in the mainstream shift to neoliberalism at least since the 1980's. Where boards of the most important museums were once old money, nobles, and other hereditary upper class, this switched to primarily the extreme rich, their families, and the direct involvement in boards by corporate representatives from giants such as Este Lauder, Goldman Sachs, etc.[2] The makeup of officers and boards will determine selection processes and juries based on preservation of the ideology and interests of the main players.[3]

THE NOBEL PEACE PRIZE

Let's have a look at another field in order to round out the argument. Who are these porcelain-skinned, benevolent Norwegians who choose warlords, homophobes and warmongers between the apparently arbitrarily chosen candidates for the "peace" award? We will tell you who: they are nationalistic, old school Norwegian aristocrats, (and a few nouveau riche duplicitously self-identifying as working class), and their main mission is to give the impression that Norway is somehow a "good guy" despite exporting primarily climate change, weapons, diseased salmon and increasingly annexing disproportional shares of world resources.[4] The Nobel jury is chosen by a mysterious ritual, taking place deep inside ornamental chambers, assisting the participants in their feeling that they are doing time-honored, legitimate work.

The legitimacy of this prize is extremely dubious, but not because their selections are so absurd, but because the selection of the jury is so comically opaque. Such anointing is as faith-based as the "white smoke/black smoke" selection of the pope by the scurrying cloaks of the papal conclave. Alfred Nobel designated in his will that a five-person jury be chosen by the Norwegian Storting, the parliament. He did not necessarily stipulate that the laureate be blatant propaganda for the sitting Norwegian government but it clearly is. The cynicism driving the ritual is overwhelmingly bleak considering its "market" is peace.

Images of the yearly ceremony from the dripping, ornamental, Oslo city hall are burned into the minds of those who have witnessed it. We couldn't believe no one in the Nobel organization felt ashamed enough to put a stop to the spectacle of people flown up from Kenya to Oslo in 2004 to dance in bright, "native" garb before the Norwegian king, queen, princesses and members of parliament all benevolently poised in their heavily decorated chairs. This display came during the supposedly progressive days of the Labor Party rule. (Open, unashamed racism publically appeared after the populist, openly xenophobic libertarian party, FrP, came to coalition power with the conservatives in 2013.)[5] Extreme racism in Norway is not confined to the extremes: scratching a political itch reached absurd levels of randomness when in 2011 the Nobel committee chose three unconnected women (Ellen Johnson Sirleaf, Leymah Gbowee, and Tawakkul Karman) apparently only because they were women of color doing something in Africa, satisfying the Labor Party's insistence on appearing worldly without taking the pains to actually understand anything at all about the world outside Norway.

GENIUS

The MacArthur Foundation fellows program is also a mysterious ritual appearing like a legitimate force majeure. Also known as the "Genius" award, the selection committee is confidential, "chosen for their breadth of experience, excellent judgment, and curiosity." While aiming for the "wide range of insightful and discerning perspectives," without defining what that could possibly mean, such a jury aims for what they already know is expected of them. "Letters of evaluation from experts in the nominee's field" tidy the process in case something unapproved slips past the gates. Furthermore, a Board oversees everything. "The Board receives for its consideration and approval the committee's formal recommendations for MacArthur Fellowships."[6] So who is this benevolent American Board who choses the jury and approves its selections? The Board is made up of deans and directors of Ivies, venture and finance capitalists, newspaper owners and, of course, former MacArthur fellows. Circular logic: the eternal mystery of genius is solved and quantified, top down! Genius is simply someone who is touched by, and thus re-confirms, the superiority of the ruling-class.

BORED AMERICA

The members of the board[7] of the Whitney Museum in New York are tai chi masters of energy displacement via social manipulation. One year the Whitney Biennial is criticized for being too New York (and Chelsea) centric, so the next one they choose curators from Chicago and London. That show is criticized for being too white, so for the next one they get two Asian American curators. With all the money and time in the world, the board of the Whitney will do what it takes to evade criticism serious enough to dismantle the façade of neutrality implied in the "country's leading survey of the most recent developments in American art."[8] We haven't yet seen any serious attempt at a class diversity show, but this may well be the duplicitous unofficial theme of the next one. The selection of artists, even when thoughtful and sincere artists are chosen by thoughtful and sincere curators, is inconsequential: the first and only selection that matters is made by the board to choose choosers who will promote and maintain the institution. Any discussion of form, aesthetic, "developments," and so-called quality is diversion. Any discussion of the artworks themselves is diversion. The purpose of the Whitney Biennial is to advance advanced neoliberal capitalism. This salon is not alone: comparable global fairs are produced with local variations of similar structures.

CRITERIA AND TALENT

In the case of the Olympics, the fastest runner is relatively easy to determine, and in physics, models are outlined by math, and this can be independently verified, and then backed by experiment. However in the case of art, there are simply no objective criteria possible without arbitrary, normative enforcement. The Salon de Paris was a normative force in the 18th to 19th centuries, inspiring artists to produce countless thousands of table settings, allegorical historicisms, and plump, frolicking, nudes. These works have aged as well as the fruit they painted. Art looks blurry in the now, denies single readings, and reinterpretation is the norm. Trompe l'oeille truly: "timelessness" is visible with the corrective lenses of the future unavailable in the present.

Talent triggers judgement so it must be demonstrated. But the demonstration of talent is amateurish, not suited to higher levels of genius. What sorts of talents need to be demonstrated in order to be recognized and awarded? Singing athletically in tune, painting a photogenic apple, tricky woodworking, and other obvious gauges of mastery are highly praised as evidence of talent although they are more often evidence of obedience, conformity, self-censorship, and ample free time — hardly qualities of genius, these are qualities of class.

Genius must be recognized, and in order for that to happen, each member of the jury must understand the stakes and be able to hear the notes that form the tune even if that tune comes from a scale they do not understand. The problem here goes far beyond the modernist issue of de-skilling, in which talent is not necessary for value (such as Kant the bad writer and Matisse the bad painter.)

Genius is often declared by people who are not themselves gifted, therefore they cannot speculate, conceptualize, or conjure what is at stake. Juries rely on connoisseurship, that is, the tasteful rendering, more or less, of what is in front of them. Adorno's brutal assessment scorched the ground experts stand on: "Connoisseurship of art is the combination of an adequate comprehension of the material and a narrow minded incomprehension of the enigma; it is neutral to what is cloaked."[9] Connoisseurship of art is familiarity without feeling or understanding essence or gestalt. Connoisseurship is pedantry. Connoisseurship is also a slight-of-hand trick used to maintain class hierarchy. Judgement by ting, ding or þing is a tiresome act with material consequences.

1. Obama's blocked Supreme Court nomination during his last days in office is an extreme example.

2. See this deeply disturbing book: Chin-Tao Wu, *Privatising Culture* (London: Verso, 2003) for a deep analysis on how, where, and when neoliberalism crept into culture management.

3. The chairs, presidents, and treasurers of the Museum of Modern Art in New York as of September 2016 are as follows: David Rockefeller former chief executive of Chase Manhattan Corporation. Ronald S. Lauder, chairman emeritus of Estée Lauder Companies. Robert B. Menschel senior director and limited partner of Goldman Sachs & Company. Agnes Gund, daughter of president of Cleveland Trust, sister of partners of Gund Investment Corporation. Donald B. Marron, chief executive officer of Paine Webber, then founder of private equity firm Lightyear Capital. Jerry Speyer, founding partner of New York real estate company Tishman Speyer. Leon D. Black, founding partner of Apollo Global Management, LLC. Marie-Josée Kravis served on the boards of the Canada/U.S. Free Trade Agreement, the Federal Reserve Bank of New York, and Ford Motor Company, and wife of billionaire financier Henry Kravis. Sid Bass, billionaire financier, former largest shareholder of Walt Disney Company. Mimmi Haas, wife of president, CEO and chairman of the Levi Strauss & Co. Marlene Hess, managing director of Global Philanthropic Services at J.P Morgan Bank, and former Director of Not-for-Profit Relations for Chase Bank. Richard E. Salomon, managing partner of investment advisory firm East End Advisors LLC.

4. The Norwegian Pension Fund owns approximately 1.3% stock of all listed companies worldwide http://money.cnn.com/2017/09/19/ investing/norway-pension-fund-trillion-dollars/index.html

5. Anna Reimann, "Did the Breivik Massacre Change Norwegian Politics?," *Speigel*, July 20, 2012. http://www.spiegel.de/international/ europe/norway-after-breivik-populists-gain-lost-ground-a-845586.html. And Alf Gunvald Nilsen, "Norway's Disturbing Lurch to the Right," *The Guardian*, 10 Sept 2013. https://www.theguardian.com/ commentisfree/2013/sep/10/norway-lurch-to-right.

6. MacAurthur Fellows, "About MacArthur Fellows Program," https://www.macfound.org/programs/ fellows/strategy.

7. Board of Trustees of the Whitney Museum of American Art is a list of plutocrats including: Co-chairmen Neil Bluhm: real estate and casino magnate; Laurie M Tisch: inheritor of great wealth; President Richard M. DeMartini: former President of the

Bank of America Asset Management Group, and partner/director of Crestview Partners financial services.

8. https://whitney.org/About.

9. Theodor W. Adorno, Else Frenkel-Brunswik, Daniel Levinson, Nevitt Sanford, *The Authoritarian Personality* (New York: Harper & Brothers 1950), 122.

FOND

Det

Det går

Det går ok

Det går så bra

Det går helt greit

Det går utrolig bra

Det går merkelig fint

Det går virkelig fantastisk

Det går virkelig så superfint

Det går utrolig superfantastisk

Det går virkelig helt utrolig flott

Det går virkelig veldig utrolig godt

Det går virkelig så helt super sprøtt bra

Det går så fantastisk dritutrolig superfint

Det går merkelig jævla virkelig dritkult godt

Det går så helt utrolig merkelig jævla superfint

Det går helt super jævla utrolig fett merkelig bra

Det går så helt superfantastisk merkelig veldig dritbra

A BINARY

The minor gestures of the minor arts: gods and treasuries tumble, all that remain are pottery shards and paving stones — seeds of consciousness from one present to a far away other.

The internet contains some art, but does not identify itself or most of its content as art. This is not for lack of ambition, but rather the reverse: the internet is much bigger than art. If the planet remains habitable, the image of the present civilization will be held within the internet for the scrutiny of future humans. This is not all bad, considering the wide spectrum available there. The internet is among the most important cultural productions in human history due to its size and range. However, the internet, with its protocols of exchange, storage, and access, does not replace art completely, not yet.

The foremost question needs to be asked continuously: what is art (today, right now)? According to the dominant model formed by Duchamp already a century ago, art is whatever the artist declares. This declaration has produced wave after wave of gestures, and filled a century of art institutions with artefacts. Even old art stands at the service of readymade contemporary branding! If everything and anything can be art, then the only question becomes an ontological binary: art or not art? How does something that is not art, become art? The self-declarative pass is deceptively simple: anyone can be an artist, and everything can be art, but there is only room for a tiny fraction of professional artists in the social hierarchy of professional art. So while everything is potentially art, and everyone can potentially be an artist, this is not true at all, and everyone understands this. Art is middle managed. Sunday hobbyist painters and junk collectors, etc., remain outside, firmly not art. Who has the appointed right as King Midas to turn porcelain and meme into gold? The manufacture of an artist uses precise social algorithms. The binary art/

not art is a strict social process, despite mid 20th century claims that "everyone is an artist," in the utopian promise to merge art and life. This formula has closed art into an entropic end game where the chessboard gets worn through the table, and the players lose their fingers, hands, arms, but still refuse to forfeit or draw because there is always a next maneuver down to the string particle. The future will not be moved by contemporary art's stupid gestures, and the great democratic majority in the present have already forgotten about the possibility that art could still be produced today, and that art lives.

NOT ART

By volume and proportion, the largest contributors to the internet are working and middle-class people – who do not self-identify as artists – who upload billions of videos, gifs, jpegs, screenshots, threads, dumps, memes, etc., onto the servers of corporate owned, mostly for-profit websites. One such image illustrates how many countries fit inside Texas: France, Canada, and... Texas. Billions of hours of YouTube videos are uploaded, some with people saying things like "I just want to hug all of them, but that's crazy, I can't hug every cat." Raymond Williams could not have imagined the rise of social media when he wrote in 1968 about the social nature of working class culture: "Working-class culture, in the stage through which it has been passing, is primarily social rather than individual (in particular intellectual or imaginative works.) When it is considered in context, it can be seen as a very remarkable creative achievement."[1] Seen so, we understand the internet to be produced mostly by commons exchange, infinite dialogue, and voluminous sharing made possible by corporate content management systems that passively collect value. Few files on the internet have passed through the procedural management of artists or curators, thus almost none of it can be categorically named art.

The contents of the internet are mostly trivial, terrible, and mostly not art, but not because of any qualitative essence, or hardly any noticeable difference at all. Most of the content of the internet is not art because the people who make it do not call it art, do not call themselves artists, and, most importantly, are not designated artists by authoritative bodies. If pressed, the countless millions of people who make and view internet contents such as memes, gifs and videos would say Internet culture is "like" art, or "an art," turning art into an expression of consumer preference instead of an ontological category of any meaningful distinction. Art institutions also do not see the internet as art, but nervous about losing control of the most powerful cultural production of the age, they try to incorporate it somehow, often in the form of an institutionally vetted artist who is officially allowed to appropriate work from the internet, usually ironically because how else can one deal with all those cats and Russian car crashes. An example of this is called post-internet art and that means the institutional upgrading of ontologically not-art into official contemporary art, ready to be consumed by the hierarchical niche audience of the art ecosystem. The other semi-acceptable way to upgrade not-art internet work to official art is for a curator to carefully select online collections and decontextualize them in the institution: this is similar to the process of selecting outsider artists, except the massive volume on the internet demands more paring.

FREEDOM

Freedom and democracy is vaguely what the internet promised when it connected the world in beautiful anarchy after expanding past its military-industrial origins. But it soon resembled the petty structures society was used to: malls, entertainment and shopping centers, corporate journalism, exploitation, and closed circuits. Freewheeling social spaces quickly became owned, operated, and gamed for private gain. After nearly two decades of rapid development, the owners of the monetized internet are more and more miserly with the value returned for what is taken in attention, marketing, and psychological, social manipulation. Each country disciplines a slightly different mass of "netizens." In China, upwards of 700 million citizens are groomed for shopping in paternal harmony. In the US, millions upon millions of working poor, one or two pay checks or illnesses away from homelessness, produce value for the Monetized Individualized Miserly Internet (MIMI), trading memes, animated gifs and fan fiction, gaining little or nothing in return except a cure for boredom and a distraction from despair. On the MIMI the majority are there to form consumer preference groups – fan sites of commercial products – confusing this with individual expression. The MIMI is an impoverished shadow of the bigger potential mass of post-precarity, post-scarcity communication and exchange.

THE FUTURE OF THE INTERNET

Qualities of good and bad, high and low, ugly and beautiful, moral and immoral, left and right, etc., etc., are absolutely unimportant compared with the internet's value as a collected whole body of work. Facebook and Google knew this from their beginnings, and are among the world's most valuable corporations because they figured out to compile, own, and exploit this body of information by using forms of social manipulation such as marketing and addictive behaviour management. The social forms of the MIMI is the unrestrained id of people living now, made visible by distributed contagion, controlled by corporate management. As a collection, the MIMI is the most complex record of the psychology of a civilization ever produced. This role used to be played by sculpture, painting, literature, and other forms of culture previously known as art. While official art is also available online –

normally in remediation or appropriation – it makes up only one miniscule part of the massive social psyche building in the form of lives lived on the internet.

Like folk songs, myths, and the so-called minor arts of the past, individuality is lost, or unimportant. Individuality likewise is so fractional and granular on the internet, that its contributions are mostly anonymous. Like so many ancient cultural productions such as ceramics, glassware, or paving stones, most are not attributed to singular geniuses. Most work circulating on the internet is semi-anonymous, and even if sources were easy to track down, few care enough to do so. Anyway this will be anonymous in the future except as marketing myths of singular contributors (unless the blockchain fully monetizes even the meme.) This mass forms a general intellect that is neither particularly wise, nor benign, as we have seen in troll invasions, propaganda wars, misogyny, and white supremacy. Nevertheless, the battle for the hearts and minds of the digital general intellect is a matter of life and death of the present, and the detached amusement of the future humans who will diagnose our contemporary with severe metastasis, that is, if there is still a planet to support them.

WHY IS ART IMPORTANT TO DISTINGUISH

While it is likely, and even inevitable, that the future will simply toss the binary art/not art into the dustbin of history, there are some particularities about art that are worth saving because they are different, other, and distinct from other cultural productions. These differences could include the following list: 1. Art does not need to be entertainment. 2. Art does not need to be funny. 3. Art does not need to be anti-intellectual. 4. Art does not need to be peer-reviewed into normative oblivion. 5. Art does not need to be made by any particular class. 6. Art does not need to be official. 7. Art does not need to be reduced to a universally transferable protocol. 8. Art does not need a contemporary audience. 9. Art celebrates difference by example. 10. Art does not need to be moral, that is, art does not need to be lawful. 11. Art is not beyond ethics: psychopathy is thusly judged.

Art can escape the hive values of the MIMI. Since the MIMI is mostly filled with a majority who accepts manipulative, capitalist entertainment as natural and right, then much of its products are hopelessly mimetic of this brutal, normative ecosystem. There is a terrible scarcity of slow, engaged, complex, intellectual work in neoliberal capitalism. If art has any hope as an ontological category that is more than the cynical maneuvering of social warfare, it is in its desire to embody difference, alternatives and dissent that speaks proudly into the future. Without this categorical difference, the future will look back and see only the endless exploitative marketplace of the internet with only blurred footnotes.

1. Raymond Williams, *Culture and Society* (Penguin, 1968), p. 313-314.

SKILL CLASS

Work is highly valued by the middle-class. Work provides a basis of the self-definition and distinction between other classes. The work moral drives middle-class people from childhood to retirement, and this is made even more exaggerated and exploited in neoliberal capitalism. However, the middle-class work moral is also informed by ambition: one must work incrementally towards high expertise in something considered useful, and this, according to belief in the meritocracy, will propel one towards incrementally higher positions, and a good life.

Romanticized homo faber is too thoughtless and dirty: middle-class praxis involves a semi-contemplative, sanitized aesthetic. Specialized skill acquisition is a joining of the body of the working class and the mind of the ruling class. The middle-class shuns back-breaking labor while still following direction from social superiors. The middle-class is based in skilful manipulation of tiny details of the universe, while passively accepting prescriptive place.

Skill acquisition and education are still among the top vessels of middle-class social capital. Skill and education is closely related to taste, which provides the framework for distinction in class and interclass hierarchy. In urban, upper-middle-class playgrounds such as Williamsburg, Kreuzberg, Södermalm, Silver Lake, Capitol Hill, etc., middle-class youth (and precariat striving towards the values of the middle-class), are keeping busy with artisan cottage industries such as craft brewing, soap making, vegetable pickling, cabinet making, and specialized craft service industries such as beard grooming, yoga, etc. The implication is that these skilled, tattooed, culturally rich (even if economically less so) youth will apply an extra amount of their valuable time for an above average product discernable to an above average citizen. Most actual capital generated in this exchange disappears upwards, according to plan, but this hardly discourages the daily work of the middle-class artisan. The artisan in this way takes pride knowing that their alienated labor is at least more valuable than the marginalized labor (slave or near-slave) that produces most consumer products in far-away (and darker-skinned) places. The hipster value system is a highly distilled middle-class skill acquisition ethic that provides distinction and solidifies class (and thus usually "race") within neoliberal capitalism. This is in the same ecosystem as contemporary art, and they are frequently next-door neighbors.

The absolute value assigned to the busy, skilful manipulation of the universe is quite unlike many other values seen in societies that have organized themselves with different priorities, with different values such as for health, family bonds, free time, uncompetitive play and recreation, result-independent contemplation, and altruistic social relations, instead of, or at least in addition to, the busy, skilful manipulation of the universe at the service of class (and thus usually "race") permanence. Rearranged value is why, for example, that the people of Costa Rica frequently report to be among the happiest people on earth.[1]

DISCIPLINING THE CLASS

It is difficult to determine how much the value of work and skill acquisition is self-determined by the middle-class, and how much it is instilled as discipline by the ruling class. The demonstration of skill reassures the ruling class that there are no idle hands or imaginations, and affirms a market value for time. The ruling class employs a sophisticated system of control– also known as the economy — that normalises the value of work and the market. The middle-class supposedly develops and polices itself to some degree in a "free" and democratic society,[2] but this is pure ideology. The middle-class uses the working class, ignores the precariat (hoping not to become precariat themselves) and accepts and takes pride in being used by the ruling class. Usefulness provides self-worth.

MIDDLE-CLASS ART

Most university and college art programs primarily teach skill acquisition. US public universities, and average to low ranked art schools that make up the majority of such institutions worldwide, focus on skill acquisition, in standard media such as photography, oil painting, clay throwing, charcoal drawing, intaglio printing, etc. The majority of art programs teach the absolute value of skill in art. Through faculty hiring, curricula, public presentation, and resource allocation, these programs de-emphasise and de-value any other possible cultural, intellectual, and conceptual content of art. The work of art must embody the spent time of disciplined middle-class praxis, or else risk the work being judged valueless in the marketplace.

Most small and medium-weight galleries promote and sell works that highlight above-average skill to a demographic of mostly upper-middle class buyers who demand demonstrations of skill that reinforce their own disciplined work value.

Professors police skill, gallerists police skill, collectors police skill, and artists police each other's skills. If an artist wishes to participate in the middle-class art ecosystem, then they must hone and demonstrate slightly above-average skill, or risk exclusion until such skill appears in their work. Demonstrations of meticulous, above-average (thus completely average) skill is demanded in almost all contemporary art forms and trends, even "dematerialized" post-conceptual art sharply hung in galleries of higher than average social capital. There are few exceptions to this formula in the art ecosystem administered by middle-class middle management.

DE-SKILLED ARTIST
AS SWEAT SHOP OWNER

In the US only the art departments of the most prestigious universities transcend craft and its disciplined, time embedded labor. In Europe only the top art academies, mostly located in the important economic capitals of Northern Europe, require students to develop more than skills. De-skilling in art (such as Duchamp's LHOOQ) has a considerable history and still enjoys some popularity today on specific occasions, but this is de-emphasized in all but a few of the most elite art education programs, and rarely shown in average galleries. De-skilling is widely ridiculed at middle-class, middling art programs, in local gallery scenes, in most mainstream press about art (see most writing in Hyperallergic, and Art F City, etc), and is even underrepresented in top salons such as the Whitney Biennial. So how does this work? Like society as a whole, distinction is a process that stratifies artists. Artists go through many occasions of social distinction, and are force to train themselves thusly.

However, de-skilled art does regularly appear in the ecosystem, so who is allowed to produce de-skilled art, and under what circumstances, and still enjoy social reward? The ruling-class does not have to play by the same rules as the other classes, obviously. An exclusive selection of artists among the precariat and middle class is seasonally added to the exclusive club of the tiny percentage of artists who enjoy the most social and economic capital. This ruling class of artists does not have to work, labor, or acquire skills: they are allowed to practice de-skilled gestures, or simply hire everything out to the other classes. As in ancient Greece, only the most elite is allowed the luxury of "creative" leisure.

The smallest percentage of artists employ middle-class craftspeople to produce large, slick, resource-heavy, expensive looking art, marketed to the 1%, instead of the upper-middle class. Or, after an artist has been declared a genius, she can practice de-skilled art because anything she touches will turn to gold. Therefore, the most prestigious art programs such as at Yale, Goldsmiths, etc. skill is taught, but with a completely different purpose: time is free from the punch clock. Instead, these selected artists are taught to behave like the ruling class: to manage middle-class craft labor, to project ownership onto every atom in the universe, and to float above the economy, without actually touching money or any other base material with one's own hands.

These elite universities teach the most important lesson for the ruling class of any profession: how to control resources and labor pools self-interestedly. Like this, the blue-chip galleries and top salons and public commissioning bodies receive their orders of mostly monumental, spectacular, high budget works of art, commanding social and/or economic capital for the ruling-class artist, market wages (as low as possible) for the middle-class craftspeople who produce it, towards big profits for the galleries.

So when Kenneth Goldsmith advocates that his Ivy League students plagiarize, waste time on the internet, etc. this provokes the predictable shock from aging middle-class ceramics professors from state schools who read the College Art Association Journal because it insults the work moral which has given their lives its meaning. However, both are simply reinforcing the values that the university system constructs in society: extreme class stratification. Goldsmith instructs his ruling class students to act like the ruling class: they must appropriate value from the other classes, and behave appropriately as the owners of all matter. The middle-class ceramicist on the other hand values time engaged in work, and the insistence on skill as a passive self-control measure. The middle-class art teacher thusly trains middle-class (aiming) students to behave professionally in middle-class settings, thus ready-mades, appropriation, and plagiarism is mostly off limits because they are considered theft, and violate the middle-class morals of honesty. The precariat and working classes are taught that shop-lifting is punishable by extreme violence that is legally and morally enforced. An immediate death penalty is not off the table, especially for people of color, as we see in cases in Ferguson, Mo, Staten Island NY, and in the Banlieue of Paris. The upper-classes are taught on the other hand, to employ middle-management for legal, systematic kleptomania of massive, art historical proportions, and to have legal council on retainer.

PUNK ROCK

The working class has produced intensive de-skilled cultural expression at key moments in recent history. Punk rock and hip-hop channelled the alienation and anger of young working and lower-middle class kids who were smart enough to reject their social condition. These expressions ended up colonized, strip mined of their resources. The Internet provided similar catharsis for the precariat, and borrowing, sampling and gestural repurposing is the norm. Offering countless sites which to upload anger and insight, the corporatized internet enables air-tight bubbles, extracts labor value from catharsis, and provides easy to trace transparency for the police in the event of more serious mobilization, all while offering little possibility of resonance, and thus, of social change.

ARTISTS OUTSIDE

If an artist wishes to produce art outside of oppressive class value systems, with a holistic understanding of reality, then she must be aware of the how, where and why: values are constructed and enforced. One cannot simply apply labor and hope it is magically unalienated.

1. Jenn Parker, "Why Costa Rica is the World's Happies Country," *The Culture Trip*, March 5, 2017. https://theculturetrip.com/central-america/costa-rica/articles/why-costa-rica-is-the-worlds-happiest-country.

2. Milton Friedman, *Capitalism and Freedom* (Chicago: University of Chicago Press, 1962).

POST-BLEAK

It almost makes sense, if we enjoy galactic, hyperbolic inflation, to use the same name for burning celestial orbs as for temporal, spectacle clogging mortals: stars. Everyone, in their respective hemispheres, on clear nights, can look up and see the same sight: glittering stars. Everyone — rich, poor, atheist or zealot — can receive photons from the same distant points into searching eyes. Far stars are our cosmic locators, they set inertial frames of reference for our home planet, allowing us to triangulate celestial relations — locating our ephemeral presence in infinity.

The abstract analogy for individuals who are bigger than the sun is stardom: everyone can switch-on screens and flip through pages and see the same, over-saturated in-circle performing larger-than-*your*-life banality. Local near-stars are our social references — our idealized, too-real pantheon — we triangulate earth-bound relational significance by them. The stars above shine upon the stars below. There are near-stars in every country.

The origin of the English word star comes from the old English steorra, old Saxon sterro and old Norse sjarna. Its connotation meaning actors and singers performing a lead only began in 1824. Many languages use the same word for both near and far stars, Spanish for example uses *estrella*. Scandinavian languages are currently less hyperbolic, using variants of the word *kjendis*, meaning known, for near stars. Both the word star, and the word famous, suggests the tautology of the class. We return again and again to Debord's formulation "That which appears is good, that which is good appears."[1] If we continue the analogy with astronomy, we understand that there are tremendous numbers of stars that cannot be seen by the naked eye from the ground on earth. These stars are detectible by orbiting Hubble telescope, and also by speculation after measuring effects on nearby interstellar bodies.

Abstract cognition is an essential faculty of humanity. Is ego inflation another essential faculty? No contemporary earth star will be alive 90 years from the day this text was written, however their traces may glow for a while. Many celestial bodies we see up above will be busy nuclear reacting billions of years from now. There is abstraction, and then there is infinite farce.

Far-stars are massive spheres of luminous plasma, splitting atoms deep into the eternal night, giant beyond any perspective we can imagine. (Tidy rows of zeros in mathematics cannot assimilate the enormity.) Stars, and groups of them forming galaxies, are so sublime that, in comparison, the word sublime is sublimely hopeless. In sci-fi, our species imagines how we could some day use technology to approach nebula (and/or save our planet from supernova and/or from ourselves, robots, etc.) But until imagination becomes hard science, we are left drifting together, dreaming that our planet remains habitable, distracted from entropy by the mesmerizing busy-ness of near-stars.

Near-stars are earthbound, animated dust particles that do or say clever things and shake their booties deep into the solar night, as small as our perspectives, easily calculated by a petty bottom line. They have an easily identifiable talent, often signing or dancing, or only the natural good looks of youth and the magnetism of dripping social privilege.

Near-stars satisfy our pathetic need for familiar authoritarian models from which to base dreams and daily lives: as kings and holy figures fade deeper into the past, we elevate near-stars, performing pitch-perfect manipulation. Near-stars appear to be terrestrial success stories, thriving, self-actualized, but this is mostly facade, judging only by the high rates of crash-and-burn. Near-stars also realize they are replaceable, like the rest of humanity, and therefore, unless they are also psychopaths, they are desperate to hold onto something to keep them in the market. Near-stars realize they have no intrinsic value beyond quantifiable marketing, and they cannot sit alone with themselves in a room for very long. Near stars should do "something", they should entertain or something, tug our heartstrings, or something. Human beings are tools for other human beings, the nastiest of vicious circles, and as constructed as a suspension bridge looping back on itself.

Hegel's concept of beauty hinged on the idea of freedom of movement, accordingly, near-stars appear to be the ultimate in beauty. Near-stars wiggle on screens and jet-set around, seemingly everywhere at once, their image is omnipresent, and their free spirit looks boundless. However, the freedom of a near-star is illusion. Their position is bound with ultra-violent social constraints that they are contractually obliged to follow. Public opinion is less stable than rhomeson particles. Once the public eye is fixed on a star, freedom of movement ends, pinned by moral panic and obliged use-value.

A feigned meme in common-sense and politics is that human life has fundamental value in itself and that this is reflected somewhere vaguely in law, assumed in morality, or at least in the mortality tables generated by the insurance industry. This is refuted by copious contrary evidence and normalized actions of governance, administration and corporate war rooms that demonstrate repeatedly and irrefutably that plant, animal or human life has no intrinsic value in capitalism. The high road of Sunzi is pure brutality. The illusion of choice and safety lead soft-targets to believe in their purchasing power. The chosen people in capitalism are free to choose between a hundred chocolate bars, and we are free to believe that the EPA and the FCC and FDA and the EU and NATO and NAFTA and WTO, and TPP, transcribe and enforce regulations protecting the value of human life along the supply chain. The very existence of near-stars refute this. The driving motivation for anyone to strive to become a near-star is the human need for safety, dignity and respect that only comes to human life under special circumstances such as those who ride the treacherous waves of near-stardom. The compensation for a life of chronic humiliation and the illusion of dominance – that near stars know is really subservience – is V.I.P. special treatment.

Simmel noted that reality is governed by one principle: "since even objective perception can arise only from valuation — we live in a world of values which arranges the contents of reality in an autonomous order."[2] Nature, on the other hand, operates with the laws of thermodynamics, and etc. Nature does not save objects of value and destroy rubbish, it deals with all objects by the same physical laws. When the planet is an asset, the trouble in the autonomous order of capitalism is that nature does not conform to valuation.

In the middle course between speculative reason and empirical realism, hope resides far, far on the other side of a framed looking glass. Meaning resides in the deep end of unfathomably deep far-stars, and in the steam gathering on the windows of a cafe. Tragic awareness is futuristic, heroic and mundane: probability is not determinacy and predictability is outlined. The doldrums of uncluttered time frees us to speculate and dream. Time without kenophobia loosens our sado-masochistic bounds with each other. We are ordered never to be bored. We are informed unambiguously not to be idle by those idle enough to dream ever-new shackles. Thinking could lead to thinking and organizing value beyond consumer fever. Near-stars absorb the bountiful potential of boredom. Vividly imagining our sun going supernova or

Andromeda plowing sidelong into our Milky Way with the pulverizing force of legions of duodecillian nuclear explosions gives great comfort and encourages sound sleep.

Mortality is completely liberating. Contemplating it is absolutely thrilling, and also deeply boring. Through Nina Simone's bound, tragic near-stardom, she sang with incredible clairvoyance: "ain't got no money, ain't got no class, no schoolin', no friends, no nothin'. Ain't got no God, ain't got no love. And what have I got? Why am I alive anyway? Got my hair, got my head, got my brains, got my ears, got my eyes, got my nose, got my mouth, I got my smile. I've got life, I've got my freedom, I've got headaches, and toothaches, like you. I've got the life and I'm gonna keep it." The miracle of consciousness is incalculably massive compared to the feelings of airless, atomized, militarized conformity one faces when pondering the new hair-cut or epithet of a near-star, or worse, their insipid handlers. Psychopaths, monks, hermits, and unsponsored surfers are the last peaceful souls in capitalism: they realize that the true miracle is consciousness lost in unbounded space and time — and this miracle is not to be spent unwisely.

Is near-stardom and sadistic use-value the best eusociality has to offer? Or has eusociality simply eroded, (evolved?) into a total kleptocracy where the universe is valuated as far down as a price tag on the quark and a discount when the boson string falls in demand?

Sin la espuela del viento
Sobre la fronda,
Ni la estrella que quiere
Ser hoja.
Una enorme luz
Que fuera
Luciérnaga
De otra,
En un campo de
Miradas rotas.

(From Federico García Lorca's poem "Deseo")

1. Guy Debord, *Society of the Spectacle* (Detroit: Black and Red Press, 1977), 12.

2. Georg Simmel, *The Philosophy of Money* (New York: Routledge, May 24, 2011), 62.

NAKED RAINBOW

Somewhere between 2003-2013, the rainbow and gradient (R&G) became a meme used for stylish mutual recognition among glittering culturati. Its origin is hazy. It may have begun in art, fashion, design or technology, and it probably came from nostalgia for 1980's computer graphics, but it spread wildly, like most ironic and catchy things from this period, on the internet. It bloomed in storefront galleries of the new Lower East Side in New York City, in the MFA studios of leafy Yale and in the fortress of gustus at Central Saint Martin's at Kings Cross. It immediately spread to Berlin, L.A., Tokyo, Sydney, Sao Paolo, and beyond, because kids post things that then get re-posted, and global taste consciousness is highly contagious. Despite its immediate popularity, for a brief moment in MFA-time, it was a sure-fire way to demonstrate privileged insider knowledge of contemporary art and fashion. Countless artists, famous or otherwise, have used the R&G in various forms, off the top of our heads: Aids 3D, Archangel, Aurbach, Coffin, Grosse, Nicolai, Offen, Pruitt, Rondine, Rozendaal, Ruby, Tuazon, and Welling. But just as quickly, it outgrew its utility and spread too far out: the meme soon out-performed its value and began to decorate the covers of populist paperbacks and provincial posters.

But instead of fading out, R&G began to oscillate between exclusive and populist. It was just too right, too suited for contagion to give it up so quickly to the masses. Art's inner rings and the children of captains of industry continued to use the meme after it hit peak populist because it is necessary to follow and to lead at the same time. Leaders are also bound to the group: who follows who? Unlike past moments in art history where lag time is standard, R&G became a fashion meme at the exact same moment it was an art meme. People wearing jackets with gradient textile prints mingled in small galleries strewn with framed gradient prints uploading jpegs to Instagrams with gradient backgrounds.

It is difficult to locate the exact location or moment where and when the end of the rainbow touches earth.

One blog did a "thoughtful" analysis on the colors of the 2012 Frieze Art Fair: "Gradient color application is evolving from photography into ceramic and painting art work. Changing color from one shade to another creates a new and quite unfamiliar application method that bring a sense of magic and dream to the everyday."

THE PERFECT MEME

We can distinguish the R&G in its meme form by defining it as the main affect and the main feature of the image, rather than a casual depiction of sky or rainbow. Some R&G forms are taken directly from nature, while others are taken from technological interventions. Photoshop is the clean visual arbitor between a user and the natural universe.

If we define a meme as a motif that repeats contagiously through cultures, Rainbows have been meme in human culture since recorded history. Rainbows play a part of most creation myths because they are spectre and spectacular. In Australian aboriginal myths, the rainbow serpent is the creator, sustainer and destroyer of life. The Navajo creation myth describes holy immortal people who travelled by following rainbows. Buddhists see rainbows as the connection between Samsara and Nirvana. In the Bible, the rainbow is used in genesis as a symbol of the covenant from a god that promises not send killer floods to wipe out humanity again. In Hindu mythology the god of thunder and war uses the rainbow to shoot arrows of lightning.

Rainbows connect the sky with the earth. Rainbows connect the natural world with our imaginations, our dreams with reality.

Rainbows are science in action at its most pleasing, aching, aesthetic, ephemeral instant. Rainbows are visual stand-in for the relative infinity of the universe.

THE MIRACLE
OF CONSCIOUSNESS

The rainbow may have mathematic and optical explanations, but explanations of any sort cannot be fully explained, they can only be repeated. We doubt the existence of Bifröst, the bridge between Asgard and Midgard, but our capacity for disbelief is the unbelievable that nevertheless exists.

SUBLIME BATHOS

Rainbows are beauty and sublime at the same time, but only if we are so overweening to believe our judgment matters at all. Kant referred to rainbows as erscheinung, shining forth (like mirages), but only because he could not dream of the sub-nuclear physical reactions that are increasingly charted by science. Erscheinung sounds cute, like Rainbow Dash,[1] indicating Kant's limitations in both science and sociology. Kant reasoned that people reduce nature to digestible bites because everything we know about the universe we know because our sense organs turn them into electrical impulses for our brains to sort out and thus own. Rainbows are perfectly harmless demonstrations of both the natural world in action and our perceptual apparatus in action. But rainbows are not the main event: they merely suggest deeper reactions. Kant could not have understood the "pure reason" of particle physics in which fundamental bodies are not directly observable — their reactions on other bodies are denoted as potential evidence of the theoretical proposal that they exist.[2] Rainbows bridge the physical world we can observe with the infinite world of particles (and far away solar systems) that we can only imagine. Adorno: "If one seeks to get a closer look at a rainbow, it disappears."[3] After nearly a century of particle experiments, reality renders aesthetic judgment pure bathos.

Anyone using the R&G meme need not consider specific cultural, historical or physical facts. R&G links spiritual, scientific and perceptual matters in an obvious, oblivious, vacant, and mesmerising display: it is primarily a surface pleasure, and as such, highly marketable. R&G is mimesis but it is also very graphic. R&G perfectly reproduces flat, even better than a map.

When flattened into two dimensions, R&G is mimesis, aesthetic and abstraction boiled to essence. In nature, R&G sit before our eyes like non-denominational miracles screaming to be used as evidence of something greater. A gradient in nature is light across the curve of a slope, a sphere for example, as in our closest and dearest sphere, for example. A gradient in nature is the play of light and matter. A 2D gradient is a very simple abstraction of that light play — mimesis as flat symbol. A 2D gradient is a cheap reproduction of nature. A 2D gradient is beautiful because it is sensuous, and tasteful (for a time), because it is of-the-moment, a flash. However, on another level, a 2D gradient is bigger because it contains the seed of consciousness, no matter how stupid its mimesis, no matter how predictable its slavishness and no matter how cheap its social effect. A 2D gradient bridges the known, observable, physical universe with the un-observable depths that we are only beginning to grasp.

Every one of us is a miracle of chance sitting on a rock that is in itself a miracle of chance. While it appears that culture and our contra-purposive ego has somehow conquered nature, it doesn't take more than a split second of perspective to realize that our small selves dwell precariously on a flying bit of matter in the back end of the galaxy that is itself breaking apart in a lost elbow of the universe. Virginia Woolf wrote during a brief flash of peak experience: "it was all as ephemeral as a rainbow."[4]

What is the difference between the sublime and a cheap effect? Spray paint washes and tricky mood lighting is symptomatic of an absent scientific life, giving rise to wishy-washy spirituality and very loose grounding in fact. White, non-secular, upper-middle class, commercial spirituality is an insistent mood in contemporary art. The niche need to cleanse, or detoxify (or whatever), without the heavy burden of the church, is satisfied by non-secular spirituality tied in with formalism, material studies, stripped tradition, and poetic reveries, spiced with irony and/or the sublime. Affect is milked from an audience of non-denominational trustees, class violence is cleansed with humanism transcended. Contemporary Art and new age self-care are capitalism's magic potions: the relatively rich pretends the pre-rational mind's ancient promises counteract pathologies while in fact they are symptoms of the same disease, and divert profits to the same villains.

A "healing arts treatment space" and boutique located in Los Angeles, Window of the Sky's mission is to "bring people together through healing, art, education, collaboration and community." On the front page of their website is a gradient sky. In the exhibition at ICA Boston called "Pulse: Art, Healing, and Transformation", blockbuster artists "shared concern for the complex relationship between art, healing, and transformation." These are only a few in millions upon millions of examples of new age salves for sale. Such remarkably shallow rhetoric acknowledges that people are suffering en masse, under the rainbow, but it avoids naming the cause: capitalism.

1. From My Little Pony, a cartoon and toy line marketed by Hasbro.

2. https://home.cern/topics/higgs-boson.

3. Theodor W. Adorno, *Aesthetic Theory* (London: Bloomsbury Academic, 2013), 168.

4. Virginia Woolf, *To the Lighthouse* (San Diego: Harcourt Brace Jovanovich, 1989), 16.

HEALTH AND PROSPERITY IN THE AGE OF KLEPTOMANIA

Health and wellness are conditions of beauty and success, and in art, the capturing of such beauty at its peak is classical. Protest often manifests as the voluntary blockage of good health and prosperity. However, since pathological kleptomania drives a wide swath of losers into debt, overwork or idleness – and desperation – could health in fact be a possible strategy of protest?

The Greek ideals of harmony and proportion are remarkable reflections of the health of the body and the polis. However, a Hellas-centric alibi is a tired meme in western narcissism: why the insistence on perceived proximity for self-identity? Why is repetition and familiarity comforting? Yet another plunder of Greece seems tasteless after the EU and the IMF has already stripped it bare: this will not be yet another text where mythic and unsatisfying inspiration is drawn from the ancient cradle of elite democracy. Let's have a look instead at other fountains of wisdom, hidden a mouse-click away. China seems to be on the ascent to world domination, let's consider its ancient sages.

So far in this book we have yet to mention that we are artists. As artists we have more at stake than a detached observation of the issues we write about, and therefore, be warned of bias. But we would like to describe in detail at least one idea we had, and demonstrate skin in the game.

FENG-SHUI

We have invited feng shui experts to set up our exhibitions on several occasions. We are also learning to apply the principals ourselves, thanks to the Internet, which is replacing the warm-body, master-student system (losing something and gaining something else.)

When working with feng shui experts, shibboliths such as the creativity of the artist and the curing abilities of the curator are delegated to another kind of expert. No nail, light fixture, pipe, windowpane or crack can escape from totalizing meaning in feng shui or in contemporary art: but there is a thin line between practicality and ideology. Feng shui was banned during the communist Cultural Revolution, but survived in the Chinese diaspora, and has since thrived in global neoliberal capitalism because everything can be monetized, especially the immaterial.

Literally translated "wind and water", feng shui is based on the concept that home, business and burial place must be arranged in harmony with natural forces in order to maximize health. Ch'i rides the feng (wind) but is held up in shui (water). A site that attracts water will attract and hold ch'i.[1]

What is ch'i? It seems to have meant something like life energy, life breath, and vapor: an even more ambiguous vitalism. Since human life depends on fresh water supply for breath, it is pre-rational wisdom that a magic life essence would move in flowing clouds and water. What about today? Water will always be an essential basis for life, but its importance has been usurped by another liquid: capital. The flows and cycles of capital are like rainfall: some places are chronically undersupplied, and others are chronically drenched. Norway and New England get heavy precipitation. Niger is at the heart of the rapidly expanding Sahara and among the countries with lowest ranked GDP. Feng shui is adeptly adopted by today's market: the flow of ch'i has transferred to the flow of capital.

Can faith systems have a positivist measurement? Will the masses be able to tell the difference between a teleological and a mechanistic reading of the signs? Nonsense colonizes with ease and facility, fueled by the earth's most plentiful and renewable resource: stupidity.

HARMONY

There has never been a "golden age" of peace and harmony in human civilization. There has never been a time of great harmony between humans and nature. Humans were ravaged by nature until the industrial revolution when humans began to return fire, leading of course, to humans being ravaged by nature even more (cancer, hurricanes, climate change, etc). There are no "good ol' days" – paleo diets and Gardens of Eden are deeply cynical marketing. There are only brief moments, tiny pockets of thriving, accidental calm in the rough seas of human history. Potential lessons could come from studying conditions of these ephemeral, isolated, harmonic moments in order to implement and expand them. It could be a goal to generate and grow harmonic islands, to make them as structurally reproducible as possible before they are swallowed, or collapse upon themselves for the same reasons that they will always implode.

There are several conditions necessary for social harmony. First, the land and the weather must be fruitful and bearable in order to provide the essential nutrients for a population. Second, kleptomaniac and zealot neighbors who covet resources for themselves must be avoided or kept at bay. Third, there must be some quiet, relaxed, social bonds between the people that are not too dogmatic. Life must be easy to sustain, but not so easy that free time is used to develop pathological greed. Psychopaths must be managed socially, contained rather than worshiped. When a harmony oasis is surrounded by mountains or sea it is easier to defend for longer. How can we balance ourselves with nature when the continents shift violently beneath our feet, and our neighbors play road warrior on the road? It would be temporary balance, of course, the improbable balance of a few brief moments. Harmony is fleeting — rare in a soul, and rarer in a public, particularly in our over-populated present. Singularities of consciousness and the all-determining natural universe are interwoven, no matter how much effort culture makes to separate people from everything else.

The people of the Basque Country maintained autonomy for thousands of years in relative harmony thanks mostly to the fact that their villages are tucked into deep, easy to defend, rainy mountains, and their fishermen could easily pluck cod from the Bay of Biscay. Several island people survived in relative harmony, such as on Hawaii and Tasmania, before eventually being overrun by genocidal kleptomaniacs from across ponds. People thrived in the bounty of Vancouver Island for at least 14,000 years, in apparent harmony, but were periodically shaken by earthquakes and tsunamis. Are there pockets of harmony now in capitalism? If so where are they? Prenzlaur Berg, Palo Alto, Roppongi, Gangnam, Deep Water Bay, Frogner, and the Upper East Side? The minimal, Buddhist-inspired offices of Steve Jobs must have been an oasis of calm and harmony inside the maelstrom of office warfare, marketing, litigation, factory suicides, and child mineral miners. Costa Rica also seems like a pretty nice place to spend a 401(k).

CH'I CORRALLING

The infirm harmony in our present moment is the fruit of ch'i corralling. Everything is accounted for, we are all tied down to one of the few varieties of the winning ideology. Our systems have become massive, enough to invert mountain and reverse rivers. China's Three Gorges Dam altered the rotation of the earth, and moved the poles. Empire has become a word that is too small to account for the monstrous calculations of data analysis and blockchain ledgers.

The Chinese idea of the "Grand Norm" advances two theories to explain the interdependency of the human and natural worlds. First, the teleological reading that "Heaven" becomes angry and causes abnormal natural phenomena when the sovereign maintains wrong conduct. The second theory is a mechanistic reading: the sovereign's bad conduct disturbs nature resulting in abnormal phenomena. These two readings are played out in mainstream press and megachurch sermons from several ideological viewpoints. "Act of God" or "force majeure" is a legal term for things beyond human control such as floods and hurricanes. The key message from a study on Indian disasters is that so-called natural disasters are not force majeure, they are force hominis: caused or at least worsened by the stupidity and/or cruelty of humans. "When we discuss disasters, 'nature', human factors, social systems, policies, politics and poverty are inseparable."[2] Badly placed dams and dangerously located and constructed houses do not build themselves. Climate change was not set off by force majeure and inequality is clearly force hominis.

Are libertines and liberals to blame for the flooding in New York and New Orleans, or are our sovereign, decadent, orgies to blame? Zealots see premonitions and signs of God's punishment everywhere, but cannot register scientific data on how methane being released by melting permafrost in Siberia might be a bummer, even for the richest and self-medicated among them. Wall Street was hit by storm floods that scientists suggest may be caused by climate change: a mechanistic reading by the principle of the "Grand Norm," would suggest the storm was the result of imbalanced, unregulated capital and its emissions. Furthermore, the site, Manhattan, gathers too much ch'i borne by winds from Iowa and waters from the New York Harbor, one of the largest natural ports in the world.

Ch'i is about harmony, but what exactly does this word mean? The Chinese meanings of the word harmony are more differentiated and colorful than our English word stemming from the usual Greek. Harmonía, goddess of agreement, and the Greek verb, harmozo, mean to fit together, to join. Ok, that is not so interesting. Chinese however has rich variations of the word harmony: musical harmony is: 韶, amicability and neighborly is: 睦, natural harmony is: 融合, melting is: 融入, and there are many, many variations from the five root characters: róng, mù, sháo, hé, and xié. The signature ideology for Hu Jintao and communist party China is the character 和 (hé) for harmony: "a prosperous society free of social conflict." Ah yes, a society free of social conflict: how is that achieved, by restraining life's liberty of movement? By corralling living beings into aesthetic forms? By liquidating conditions for sustainable, rural, self-sufficiency in order to fill the slave factories that manufacture Silicon Valley? We are reminded again of the spectacularly grotesque Beijing Olympics opening ceremony where life was perverted into aesthetic form for viewing pleasure from high above.

To be in harmony with the present ideological universe means to be swimming in the great, heavily guarded flow of capital. Borders and trade routes run under shadows cast by nuclear arms, and militarized police guarantee the "graduated sovereignty" of citizen subjects.

AESTHETIC INSURANCE

The feng shui industry is used today by Chinese and Western believers and non-believers alike as an extra insurance policy, because, why not? Feng shui is often used to appease potential Chinese business connections, very desirable even during protectionist regimes. The feng shui industry is also successful because it spices up a blasé, banal, daily existence, much like art, with secular spirituality. Enforced liquidity is the ideal in another institution: the Kunsthalle, a non-collecting, temporary location for art. The Kunsthalle taps into world streams of ch'i, visualizing e*flux.

THE AESTHETICS OF HEALTH

A meme in contemporary art is the aesthetics of health: athletics and the body as temple lifestyle industry on display. Artists are using sports gear such as yoga mats, climbing grips, surf boards, foam bike tape, grip tape, water bottles, weight lifting gear, skateboards, and mountain climbing gear in style-altered readymades. Timur Si-Qin did a show at Société Berlin of a series of yoga mats melted on sheets of steel in summer 2013. His work is a vaguely fascist celebration of the "evolutionary psychology" of advertising, mostly involving young, beautiful and healthy bodies, a neoliberal Leni Riefenstahl. This aesthetic of anti-critical market conformism justified by selected, perverted snippets of science and philosophy (scientific racism, along with the ubiquitous, extremely reactionary, market-friendly readings of Object Oriented Ontology,)[3] is widespread in the elite braches of the art ecosystem. Pamela Rosencranz regularly shows brand name water bottles filled with different shades of skin-colored cream and stretched "high tech" sports fabric smeared with the same cosmetic. Roman Signer has used broken, sectioned or stressed canoes since at least the 1980's. Bicycle gear reached a particularly hot moment around 2012, because of its slick, customizable, abstract details such as highly coordinated color combinations and pattern trim highlights in individualized, aestheticized, hi-tech materials. Speaking at length with one young Norwegian artist, we assumed he approached his hyper masculine, sexualized bicycle gear, eye-candy sculptures, with some criticality or irony of the health industry. It took us a few minutes to realize that neither he nor his work were ironic or critical in the slightest. He was legitimately in love with his expensive bicycle and all its trimmings, his peak experience was to cruise the streets of Oslo, flexing his muscular legs. Who can blame him? Health and physical beauty is wonderful, the most desirable part of life, and the primary marketing tool for everything. Health is also very expensive: it is to die for.

Is punkish self-destruction an aesthetic protest anymore? The busy-ness vile-maxim is rock n roll destruction of health and well-being on an epic, worldwide binge. So wouldn't health and prosperity be the appropriate protest? Perhaps, but a healthy worker is an ideal, mute citizen running the hamster wheels in gyms overlooking the corralling of ch'i on busy-ness street corners of our great cities. The busy-ness of health is a luxury for those who do not themselves labor in order to eat. Finally, ultimately, capital does not care whether consumers (aka people) are alive or AI, healthy or plague-ridden. If a market begins to contract, capital is shifted to the next battlefield, strategically repositioned by healthy, yoga practicing middle-managers who market product grades to all levels of health and prosperity.

SUN AND SHADE

In summer 2011, we asked feng shui master Pun Yin to do the lay
out of our exhibition in New York. She had never worked with an
art exhibition, although she had worked with big business and
big government — Donald Trump,[4] Mayor Bloomberg, and the
New York City Health and Hospitals Corporation were among
her clients. (She has also been on Fox news and the Conan O Brian Show, the latter using humorous condescension, the former
respectfully condescending.) We had a tiny budget, but Pun Yin
was curious about the art world so she agreed to work with us for
a discount price.

Yin and yang find their earthly connections in measurements
of sun and shade. Life is possible with the correct proportion of
sun and shade. It is possible, thanks to technology and resource
exploitation, that a metropolis such as Dubai can exist in a burning desert, and that frozen, bleak Oslo is among Europe's fastest
growing capitals. The balance of sun and shade is shifted by using air conditioning systems and air-conditioned supply trucks
running distribution patterns of air conditioned trucks carrying
air conditioning units to air-conditioned supply centers. Yin and
yang is essential in feng shui — life needs the correct proportion
of sun and shade. Furthermore, the 5 elements must be balanced
for harmony. Improbable harmony makes life possible, for real:
this is more than vitalism or literary cleverness. Scientifically, if
we don't have all our internal physical systems running smoothly,
in a suitably mild climate, our lives will end within moments.
Likewise, food can be shipped up to frozen Oslo, but as soon as
the oil fund runs dry and distribution networks shift to avoid the
bankrupt place, its population will drain out, and life will shift
elsewhere. Oslo before too long will look like a drab, corporate
Herculaneum for archeologists to sift through.

CH'I CORALLING

The ideal busy-ness sees the prosperous flow of ch'i corralled ever upwards. Motion, flow and non-stop turnover are ideal in feng shui and ideal in busy-ness governance applied to every facet of life. Precarity is encoded into law. Property taxes in the United States, (and many countries, even socialist ones,) to give one example, are designed so that no one actually owns their own property, even if there is no mortgage or landlord. Taxes on the total value of a property are assessed by formulas called millages, and they are a means of taxation to have resources for public works and infrastructure such as schools, instead of relying on the prosperity of robust income and corporate taxes that refract the flow of ch'i. Since property taxes can be many thousands of dollars per year per dwelling, or more for places zoned for business, this means that there must always be economic activity connected with any property, big or small, commercial or domestic. We see a particularly insidious chain of events in Detroit and other cities with large populations of precariat (mostly black) homeowners who are forced out of their long-term homes to make way for "urban revivals" and "developments" because they can't afford rising property taxes. There must always be a flow of ch'i coming into and out of all properties in the United States or else they will be "foreclosed" upon by local governments. The person who otherwise owned the property outright will be forced into homelessness due to blockage of ch'i, if they lose their job, if their busy-ness falls out of favour with the masses, etc. It becomes exaggerated and extreme in "developing" urban areas when property values shoot to the moon resulting in cities filled with the most economically "productive" activities. This is a simple means of control using the rhetoric of the flow of ch'i for the health of the community. U.S. property taxes make explicit that there is no space for failure, dissonance, experimentation, reflection, protest, simple living, or other bad or blocked ch'i. (Remember that tax-exempt not-for-profit status is highly regulated, and forbids "political activity.") People or activities not following the legislated flow of ch'i cannot maintain a space of their own, and are forbidden to rest in place, in health or harmony.

One argument that the opponents of The Patient Protection and Affordable Care Act (aka "Obamacare") provisions came up with is that "that they are beyond the scope of Congress's power to regulate interstate commerce because they regulate inactivity (declining to purchase health insurance,) as opposed to regulating economic activity."[5] This interesting implication reminds us that in neoliberalism, law is used to enforce flow: there can be no still water. Ch'i must flow. The mandate of a nation to care for every person within is replaced by the mandate that every person must hustle, churning in place, or else face unspeakable penalties.

Another busy-ness location where the flow of ch'i is coralled ruthlessly is in education. In busy-ness education, students and teachers should flow freely without the burden and bind of security or an image of the future. The architecture of education ensures the direction of the current. Tenure is now won like a lottery. Even in Scandinavia local governments have removed tenure from the art academies, leaving professors of art to flow around with limited contracts, uprooting any possibility of solid connection to the community or to grow within the institution. The U.S. adjunct teacher strategy is the same but with rock-bottom working conditions: adjuncts are "incentivized" to flow out of their awful, overworked, precarious situation. And in much of the westernized world, the protagonists in education – the students – flow through the edu-factories, human rivers of ch'i, liquidity corralled into pre-determined class stratifications, yoked with securitized debt.

TRADITIONAL KNOWLEDGE
CORRALLED

Traditional knowledge can be a lucrative market, especially when it is health related; yoga is another of many examples. But while capitalism can revive ancient forms, it does so by freeze drying and packaging traditional knowledge as intellectual property to be owned like lumps of gold. The kleptomaniac content industry attacks the public domain with waves of legal attacks supported by government, thanks to relentless industry lobbying. Disney lifted folk tales from the public domain and then blocked them off with copyright claims, and lobbied congress to extend copyright terms, etc. etc.[6] Facebook polices the words "face" and "book." Usage of basic words such as Apple or Alphabet are restricted, and the list grows daily.

The California "master" Bikram Choudhury, self-proclaimed Hollywood "yoga teacher to the stars," used the U.S. legal code to claim his "intellectual property" — ancient yoga poses. Bikram's claims are historically, ethically, aesthetically, intellectually, scientifically, logically, ontologically, and categorically invalid, in every way, but that did not stop his legal team from extorting "settlements" from those without the legal resources to fight him. In 2012, after years of legal limbo, the U.S. copyright office finally woke up, ruling that ancient yoga sequences are not protected by copyright as it is currently written.[7] World copyright and patent offices are taking notice of India's bold move to fight chi coralling of traditional knowledge, by assembling the Traditional Knowledge Digital Library, a database of 1200 Ayurvedic, Unani and Siddha Formulations assembled and searchable in order to invalidate biopirating and bioprospecting by establishing prior art evidence easily read by judges. For example, a record from 2013 lists an abandoned patent application to the U.S. Patent office for the use of hing spice as an "agent for expelling parasites in humans, animals or birds." Comfortably in the public domain, we can all freely sprinkle hing (asafetida) to expel parasites such as Bikram from our system.

CHARTS

Master Pun Yin arrived in the Dumbo art space with our personal charts in hand after having spent the previous evening consulting her books. Personal charts are important in feng shui to determine harmony and the occupant's innate compatibility with the space. Alejandra's chart said she was missing metal, the curator was missing wood and Aeron's chart was perfectly balanced, missing nothing — very unusual according to Pun Yin. Alejandra needs to wear metal jewelry for the rest of her life. (Interesting because she is allergic to metal, her skin turns grey and breaks out in rashes.) Everything in the space can be altered and adjusted for harmony except one thing: Alejandra is the sign of the snake and Aeron is the sign of the boar — mortal enemies. Pun Yin glanced up at us with deep disapproval, but she maintained a respectful silence. We have been together since 1995.

After a reading of the space itself, it was determined that our work needed very specific organization in order for balance to be achieved. A composition of upward motion assists the dynamic flow of ch'i, and demonstrates creativity. Upward motion can be simulated with angles and triangles, therefore, we should arrange our works in these shapes. She also recommended certain of our more fragile works should be protected by using solid colors on the floor, punctuated with flowers. But nothing could be done about the building itself. Homes and businesses should not be under bridges, ch'i is whisked this way and that.

Dumbo, the branded neighborhood, got its name from being under the Manhattan Bridge, although it is also under the Brooklyn Bridge. Pun Yin, the pragmatist, said that the entire neighborhood absorbs the bad ch'i generated by being under these two massive bridges, and there is really nothing that could be done about it from a feng shui perspective. The giant white column in the center of the exhibition space, on the other hand, structural support for when commodities were stored within the city, could be countered by painting it gold. Pun Yin strongly suggested this giant would become invisible. Our show looked great after Pun Yin was done and several visitors remarked that the art center had never looked better. However Dumbo Art Center would be closed a year later, an invisible non-profit in the middle of New York's ch'i typhoon.

Pun-Yin wrote:
"FIRST & most UNIQUE exhibition in New York EVER ~ Art & Feng Shui collaboration of 3 world renowned masters who convey energy through history, textures, east meets west contents, old & new techniques for the 21 century. The exhibition by Aeron Bergman and Alejandra Salinas will be placed in cohesion to the art of Authentic Chinese Feng Shui by the reigning Feng Shui master of the world – Master Pun-Yin who brought Feng Shui into mainstream America and internationally since the early 90's. This exhibition would truly be a unique experience of all senses because you would be enveloped with "harmony in detail." Master Pun-Yin's solid reputation for helping to turn the fortunes of her high profile clients around since the early 90's documented by the int'l press. FORTUNE Magazine in 1996 wrote that "her work marks a new nexus between this country's corporate and metaphysical sectors."

For more info. please visit www.punyin.com

1. Fung Yu-Lan, *A Short History of Chinese Philosophy* (New York: Macmillan Company, 1948)

2. Unni Krishnan, S. Parasuraman, "India Disasters Report II: Redefining Disasters," Oxford University Press (2013).

3. We can imagine the exuberant scene of the board meeting at Nestle when it was excitedly announced that there is a para-academic movement afoot that grants objects, such as jars of instant coffee and bottles of privatized tap water, the same legal, social and philosophical status and rights as human beings.

4. This was written before Trump was elected president on a platform that, among other things, railed against trade with China despite having actively done so himself.

5. Jedediah Purdy & Neil S. Siegel, "The Liberty of Free Riders: The Minimum Coverage Provision, Mill's 'Harm Principle,' and American Social Morality," *American Journal of Law & Medicine*, 38 (2012): 374-396.

6. See Lawrence Lessig's books for more.

7. Federal Register, Vol. 77, No. 121. June 22, 2012. http://www.copyright.gov fedreg/2012/77fr37605.pdf.